HERITAGE THAT HURTS

HERITAGE, TOURISM, AND COMMUNITY
Series Editor: Helaine Silverman
University of Illinois at Urbana-Champaign

Heritage, Tourism, and Community is an innovative new book series that seeks to address these interconnected issues from multidisciplinary and interdisciplinary perspectives. Manuscripts are sought that address heritage and tourism and their relationships to local community, economic development, regional ecology, heritage conservation and preservation, and related indigenous, regional, and national political and cultural issues. Manuscripts, proposals, and letters of inquiry should be submitted to *helaine@uiuc.edu.*

The Tourists Gaze, the Cretans Glance: Archaeology and Tourism on a Greek Island, *Philip Duke*

Coach Fellas: Heritage and Tourism in Ireland, *Kelli Ann Costa*

Inconvenient Heritage: Erasure and Global Tourism in Luang Prabang, *Lynne Dearborn and John C. Stallmeyer*

Heritage That Hurts: Tourists in the Memoryscapes of September 11, *Joy Sather-Wagstaff*

HERITAGE THAT HURTS

Tourists in the Memoryscapes
of September 11

Joy Sather-Wagstaff

Left
Coast
Press
inc.

Walnut Creek, California

Left Coast Press is committed to preserving ancient forests
and natural resources. We elected to print this title on 30% post
consumer recycled paper, processed chlorine free. As a result,
for this printing, we have saved:

2 Trees (40' tall and 6-8" diameter)
1 Million BTUs of Total Energy
203 Pounds of Greenhouse Gases
976 Gallons of Wastewater
59 Pounds of Solid Waste

Left Coast Press made this paper choice because our printer,
Thomson-Shore, Inc., is a member of Green Press Initiative,
a nonprofit program dedicated to supporting authors, publish-
ers, and suppliers in their efforts to reduce their use of fiber
obtained from endangered forests.

For more information, visit www.greenpressinitiative.org

Environmental impact estimates were made using the Environmental Defense
Paper Calculator. For more information visit: www.papercalculator.org.

LEFT COAST PRESS, INC.
1630 North Main Street, #400
Walnut Creek, CA 94596
http://www.LCoastPress.com

ISBN 978-1-59874-543-6 hardcover
ISBN 978-1-59874-544-3 paperback

Library of Congress Cataloguing-in-Publication data:

Sather-Wagstaff, Joy.
Heritage that hurts: tourists in the memoryscapes of September 11 /
Joy Sather-Wagstaff.
   p. cm.—(Heritage, tourism, and community)
   Includes bibliographical references.
   ISBN 978-1-59874-543-6 (hardcover: alk. paper)—ISBN 978-1-59874-544-3
   (pbk.: alk. paper)
1. Heritage tourism. 2. War memorials. 3. Holocaust memorials. 4. September 11
Terrorist Attacks, 2001. I. Title.
   G156.5.H47S37 2011
   306.4'819—dc22
                              2010044938

Printed in the United States of America

♾™ The paper used in this publication meets the minimum requirements of
American National Standard for Information Sciences—Permanence of Paper for
Printed Library Materials, ANSI/NISO Z39.48–1992.

To Sean Sather-Wagstaff

Contents

Illustrations

Preface

Although some people may feel uneasy with researching and writing about 9/11, an event that, for some, is still "too close to be real history," Geoffrey White argues that "it is just such a fluid moment of contested meaning making that anthropology would be expected to embrace" (2004:293). In my work at and beyond the World Trade Center (WTC), I took on the challenge of tracing the process of contested meaning-making as it transpired through multiple constructive, performative acts, particularly acts that were largely unacknowledged—those of tourists at and beyond the site. I sensed a unique opportunity to understand how official, public, and vernacular individual memories and histories are constructed and the many ways in which they are in dialog with one another across space and time. As an ethnography of commemorative place-making and the relationships between official, public, and vernacular memory and history, this work contributes to a richer understanding of the multiple ways in which commemorative sites, both landscapes and museums, are socially made and remade while constantly remaining places for diverse and often highly contested meanings.

The various paths that led me to the research resulting in this book are circuitous but deeply intertwined. I attempt to unravel at least part of their "knottiness" here. Why do I study tourists and travel? Travel is something that has significantly shaped who I am. Childhood vacations in my home state of Texas were spent visiting Cowtown, camping in national parks, walking the historical Galveston boardwalk district, and riding roller coasters at Six Flags, so named for the six flags that have flown over the territory now known as Texas. I began traveling internationally at age 11, first as a performer/tourist, then as a businessperson/tourist, and, in the present, as scholar/anthropologist/tourist. From Lisbon to Marseille, Havana to Dublin, and Taipei to New York, travel is a practice that has repeated itself throughout my life, albeit far too infrequently for my own tastes. My travel, regardless of reason and motivation, has always involved touristic activities—visiting museums, cemeteries, theme parks, sites of historical events, art galleries, churches, restaurants serving local specialties, and exceptional (and many not-so-exceptional) examples of architecture. Well before my career as an academic, I had already seen many commemorative historical sites, including Hiroshima, Auschwitz-Birkenau, Pearl Harbor, Dealey Plaza, Checkpoint Charlie, and more, some of which I write about or reference in this work. So, as a tourist, I am performing an unusual sort of native anthropology.

Until September 11, 2001, my research focused on several dimensions of tourism and the fine arts in Havana, Cuba. Blending my interests as an anthropologist, a tourist, and an artist, I found the complex, highly political processes of creating cultural patrimony for both local and tourist consumption fascinating. I returned to the United States from Havana in July of 2001 at the end of a summer fieldwork period, pondering the viability of my research there under the still difficult and precarious political, social, and economic conditions of the not-quite post–Special Period era. Then September 11, 2001, happened. The events of that day changed many peoples' lives in many ways, and my own life was no different. I lost no one that day, but several people I know and love did lose someone near and dear. But as horrified as I was and continue to be by the events and aftermath of this day, I was, and still am, equally inspired to try to understand something about the vast and complex processes of recovery and remembrance. I changed my research to focus on this process as viewed through the lens of tourism and the experiences of tourists from around the United States and beyond. This was a perspective largely missing from the existing literature on commemoration and historical site-making and one rarely considered directly in the array of scholarly articles and books on 9/11 that emerged very shortly after the attacks.

My fieldwork in New York City began in the summer of 2002 and continued every summer through 2004. I returned every year through 2007 for the anniversary, visiting for several days before and after September 11th. I spent time in Oklahoma City at the Oklahoma City National Memorial and Museum during 2002 and 2009, and off-site fieldwork took place 2002–2009 as I followed up with tourists I met in Manhattan as well as engaged with returned tourists in the towns where I lived and live and literally everywhere I went. It was a deeply rewarding research project on many levels. However, it was not entirely exempt from a range of personal difficulties, political challenges, and ethical issues that were not entirely dissimilar from some of those that faced me while doing work in Cuba.

Thus I must speak to the difficulties and issues involved in doing ethnographic research under conditions of war, both unofficial and official. In retrospect, I simply moved from doing research under the conditions of one war, the last gasps of the Cold War, to a new one, one that began with the first Gulf War in the 1990s and came back to life in fits and starts beginning on September 12, 2001, leading to the October 2001 invasion of Afghanistan and in 2003, the second Gulf War. Doing anthropology under any conditions of war is challenging and should be discussed openly and honestly, particularly in terms of how such conditions affect us personally, affect our research environments, and affect the ways in which our research and written work may be interpreted in the future. Ethnography is indeed a form of historiography, and if for no other reason than this, some transparency is in order.

The conditions in Manhattan were always potentially dangerous, be it real or imagined danger. I was rerouted a number of times during my subway commutes to the WTC site as main hub stations were closed down because of "unidentified objects" that required examination by the police, fire department, and SWAT teams. More than once I was surprised to end up in Brooklyn when I knew I was on a train going to a different destination. It was common to encounter groups of police wearing the city equivalent of combat gear—full-body bulletproof armor, strike helmets, huge rifles. At one point I found myself trapped for a short time in the Century 21 department store on Church Street, directly across from the WTC site. A bomb threat had been called in to a location just south of the site, and the department store closed every exit except for the one on Broadway, to the east. A line of hundreds inched slowly toward the lone door while store employees refused to provide an explanation, leaving us extremely uncomfortable and trying to remain calm. I found out about the reason for the lockdown later that night on the evening news. Just as the locals dealt with these events, bouncing back and going about their business, so did I.

I was able to freely do immersive fieldwork around Manhattan and the WTC site under post-9/11 conditions of surveillance and the progression of military actions from Afghanistan to Iraq because I do not fit the stereotyped profile of a terrorist. Although carrying a camera marked me as "likely to be a tourist" and few people noticed that I was taking as many photos of those engaging with the site as I was of the landscape, this invisibility was not unproblematic. As a fair-skinned, blond female, I was far less likely than others engaging in similar photographing activities to come under serious scrutiny for or be restricted in my activities. My appearance facilitated the privilege of being able to spend several hours a day for continuous weeks and months at and around the WTC site without being suspected of collecting images and information that, according to the U.S. Department for Homeland Security and the Patriot Act, could be interpreted as useful for planning terrorist activities.

However, other amateur and professional photographers across the country were not so lucky. Mostly male and non-white, a number were arrested or harassed for taking photographs in places considered of possible terrorist interest (such as bridges, power plants, skyscrapers, and mass tourism destinations) in New York,

Colorado, Oregon, Maryland, Pennsylvania, and California.[1] Because of my appearance and despite the fact that there are surveillance cameras throughout the WTC area and Manhattan, I was never once questioned about my very regular presence at the site nor was I ever the focus of police attention as a possible criminal danger to tourists in the manner that young males of color at the site sometimes were. If I were brown-skinned and dark-haired (male or female but especially male), I would seriously doubt that I could have been able to complete my work without someone, somewhere, questioning me—or worse. Simply being able to *do* research without harassment was a result of my white privilege but one that was not, perhaps, a typical scenario of how such privilege enables scholarly research.

Working at the WTC site was often difficult, given that some of the tourists and locals that I met held and actively expressed ethnocentric, jingoistic, conservative, and/or extremely radical political positions that conflicted with my progressive political identity. In our conversations I frequently found myself going back-and-forth between attempting objectivity and challenging my participants' perspectives. More important, such encounters also challenged me to not prejudge my ethnographic subjects but instead struggle to make sense of their positions through ongoing engagement. As an anthropologist I ought not privilege my own subjectivity over those of my participants but instead take their positions seriously—I may critique them but not override their sentiments with my own in the process of my analysis. The insights provided through my continued engagements with participants enabled me to see somewhat more clearly how such subjectivities are constructed and perhaps, just maybe, how to provide a few possibilities for working toward broader social change when it comes to the pervasive ethnocentrism and racism that underlie so much violence and tragedy in the world.

This work was also emotionally challenging. Imagine doing fieldwork where at least once a day someone bursts into uncontrollable tears; on some days I was that person, but more often my participants were the ones. The stories I heard from locals, survivors, victims' family members and friends, rescue workers, and tourists alike were painfully heart-wrenching. I still feel ill-equipped, unprepared, and too awkward emotionally to represent many of these stories, and I hope that I have done justice to the ones I do retell here. Perhaps in the future, when more time has passed, I will be able to tell those that do not appear in this book. These stories made it clear to me that most of the world was connected to the events of 9/11 in some manner and that their telling and retelling, tears and all, is indeed a fundamental part of writing, figuratively and literally, the diverse histories of September 11, 2001, even as they continue to unfold in the present.

ACKNOWLEDGMENTS

I am deeply indebted to everyone who participated in my research—the hundreds of tourists who freely gave their time while on vacation and locals from the New York City area and around the United States who told me stories I will never forget. Thanks to my friends, family, tourists, and colleagues, who constantly sent me news articles, commemorative items, and memorial websites from all over the world. Special thanks go to the directors, curators, and collections managers of the Oklahoma City National Museum and Memorial who worked with me and welcomed me so warmly as an on-site researcher and continued to be long-distance resources over the years when I could not visit in person.

So many mentors and colleagues have been critical to my research and writing; if I fail to include some of you here, please accept my apologies and my deepest thanks. I thank Ed Bruner and Arlene Torres for providing incredible intellectual stimulation, guidance, and mentorship from the earliest days of my academic career. Helaine Silverman, editor of this Left Coast Press series, has been a constant source of support for my research, and I am thankful that she has always seen value in it, even when I questioned its significance. Brenda Farnell and Janet Keller encouraged me to think outside the box about both research methods and ethnographic writing. The constructive criticism and rich conversations generated by my fellow participants in the Illinois Program for Research in the Humanities 2003–2004 Fellows Seminar on the theme of violence greatly shaped this work from its earliest stages and in more ways than I ever imagined possible.

Funding from the University of Illinois at Urbana-Champaign and North Dakota State University supported much of the field research for this project and the writing process. Special thanks go to Angela Glaros, Emily Hagemeister, Rachel Leibowitz, Ellen Moodie, Jen Shoaff, Rebekah Sobel, Adam Tyma, Sujey Vega, and Christina Weber for an array of support, from reading drafts to intense and constructive conversations on our research projects. I am especially grateful to Mitch Allen at Left Coast Press and Stacey Sawyer for her wonderful copyediting work.

CHAPTER 1

Introduction

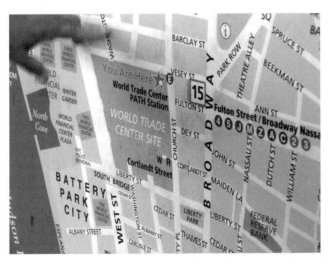

Figure 1.1 Manhattan map at the World Trade Center visitor's kiosk
(© Joy Sather-Wagstaff 2004)

"YOU ARE HERE": CONSTRUCTING A HERITAGE THAT HURTS

Tragedy—human death and injury, the physical destruction of buildings and landscapes, and the psychological and social

19

dissonance that results—is processually transformed into memory and historicity through the social production, construction, performance, and consumption of commemorative sites for what John Schofield, William Johnson, and Colleen Beck describe as "a heritage that hurts" (2002:1).[1] Commemorative sites are not automatically sacred or otherwise historically important simply because a disastrous event occurred; they are spaces that are continuously negotiated, constructed, and reconstructed into meaningful places through ongoing human action. Although usually understood as static places of "official" cultural expressions of history and memory, particularly when fully formalized with museums, monuments, and memorial landscapes, these sites both generate and are informed by what John Bodnar defines as "public" and "vernacular" history and memory through polysensory human engagement with the places themselves (1992:75).

Public memory and history "emerge from the intersection between official [dogmatic, homogenous, and authorized] and vernacular [multiple, ambiguous, local, and heterogeneous] cultural expressions" (Bodnar 1992:13). Public memory also mediates between dominant, official (and usually national) narratives and local or individual narratives, and it is also a means of accepting, resisting, informing, or even significantly altering these official histories and memory. It is largely through tourism that commemorative and other historical sites act as places where these official, public, and vernacular histories and memories intersect and act in dialog. Visiting sites of tragedy and death is not only a way for people to question the "mythic underpinnings of society" (Kugelmass 1994:178); in the process people make the sites historically salient in official, public, and vernacular memory across communities of belonging, both imagined (Anderson 1991) and lived in the everyday.

The events of September 11, 2001, continue to endure in cultural memory for many as an unexpected, violent rupture in everyday life that forcefully marked the transition from the 20th to the 21st century. The events and aftermath of that day are the focus of my study, specifically as they are represented in the commemorative site-in-process that has been and will remain the shifting World

Trade Center (WTC) landscape until the formal memorial land-scape and museum are completed. In my research I focused on the on- and off-site experiences and memories of a broadly dispersed public as represented by tourists who visited New York City during 2002–2009 and their role in the making of the WTC commemorative site. To focus on tourists enables an understanding of how violent events of scale are culturally mediated through time and space, the generative, everyday relationships between collective and individual agents in the production of historical consciousness, and the socially constructive roles that visual and material culture and embodied experience play for memory-making in an age of mass production and consumption.

This ethnography goes a bit of the way to meeting anthropology's ongoing challenge to "illuminate, inform and expand the possibilities of personal, social and political responses to 9/11" (Clarke 2004:10), representing only a very minute fraction of the many narratives of 9/11. These stories are continually unfolding histories-in-process, and although the events of and responses to 9/11 are perhaps the most documented of any disaster of scale in human history to date, the struggle and challenge to make sense of them continue. As a scholar in a largely interpretive social science subdiscipline, I join others across disciplines in a commitment to generate a much-needed "critical, humane discourse that creates sacred and spiritual spaces for persons and their moral communities, spaces where people can express and give meaning to the tragedy [of 9/11] and its aftermath . . . connecting the personal, the political, and the cultural" (Denzin and Lincoln 2003:xv). A wide range of valuable public and scholarly projects on 9/11 have already been undertaken. Through this book I add more stories, voices, and perspectives—both mine and my participants'—to this growing body of works.

This book's contribution is built on the fact that (to my knowledge), no scholars have looked specifically at *tourists* as a primary, relevant population for study that focuses on 9/11 commemorative sites. In general, when tourists to the WTC site are mentioned in the media and by scholars, they are usually disparaged and criticized, framed as profaning the "sacred site" with their touristic activities.

Yet tourists not only are directly and indirectly providing economic support for commemorative sites worldwide, they also are the population that geographically disperses knowledge of these sites through the narrative, performative, and visual culture of travel once off-site, post-visit. In the case of 9/11 they also represent what sociologist Kai Erikson identifies as the "hinterland" population of the United States and beyond, one that has been far less studied than persons in and around New York City yet who nonetheless "feel that they were witnesses *to*, victims *of*, even actors *in*" the event (2005:354). I therefore consider tourism to be a significant part of the cultural terrain through which tragic events past and present are apprehended, comprehended, and commemorated.

This book presents a deeper understanding of the social, political, and emotional effects and consequences of violent events that reverberate far beyond the physical sites where they occurred and in the process reveal the constructive roles that tourists play in making the diverse and often contested meanings accorded to historical commemorative sites. Although my primary focus was on 9/11 sites, my study is contextualized within a range of contemporary commemorative sites that have been formalized or, like the WTC site, are still in process. The Oklahoma City National Memorial plays a significant comparative role as a formalized site, as does the Vietnam Veterans Memorial in Washington, D.C. Both sites have greatly influenced the cultural templates for the formal WTC memorial landscape and museum, other 9/11 memorial landscapes, and the various commemorative practices performed by locals and tourists at the WTC and other sites of disaster, tragedy, and death. Like the WTC, both sites are also tourist destinations, and the Oklahoma City site is one that depends heavily on tourism for its existence, both economically and as a site that continues to develop its historical saliency as one of the most devastating occurrences of terrorism on U.S. soil.

"WE'VE BEEN ATTACKED . . ."

On the morning of September 11, 2001, millions of people saw or heard what transpired as it happened. Many in Manhattan and the surrounding areas witnessed the events at the WTC first-hand—some never survived to tell us what they saw. Those of us at a geographical distance from the disastrous events occurring in New York, Pennsylvania, and Washington, D.C. were second-hand witnesses, watching in shock as the events unfolded on television and were replayed over and over on nonstop news broadcasts. American Airlines Flight 11 from Boston, the first of four airplanes highjacked by members of Al-Qaeda, an Islamic extremist organization, crashed into the north tower of the WTC at 8:45 A.M. Eastern Standard Time. Eighteen minutes later, United Airlines Flight 175, also from Boston, crashed into the south tower. By 9:21, with both towers burning, flames and smoke visible from miles around, all New York and New Jersey airports had been shut down and all bridges and tunnels in the area closed to further ground traffic.

Twenty minutes later, all United States airports' flight operations were stopped and all inbound trans-Atlantic flights rerouted to Canada. American Airlines Flight 77 crashed into the Pentagon at 9:43—it originated at Washington, D.C.'s Dulles International Airport only a few miles away—and the White House was immediately evacuated. At 10:05 millions watched in stunned horror as the south tower of the WTC collapsed. Five minutes later, United Airlines Flight 93 from Newark, New Jersey, crashed near rural Shanksville in Somerset County, Pennsylvania. The north tower of the WTC collapsed at 10:28. It was noon before American Airlines and United Airlines confirmed the loss of all four of the highjacked flights. At 5:20 Building 7 of the WTC collapsed after sustained fires and debris from the fall of the north tower had weakened the structure.

In all, four of the seven WTC buildings (1, 2, 3, and 7) were nearly or completely destroyed in a matter of hours, and the remaining three (4, 5, and 6) were so badly damaged that they were later demolished.[2] Thousands of local and nonlocal professional rescue workers and volunteers worked feverishly at the WTC site through September in the hopes of finding survivors, yet very few were found. Fires at the site burned until December, and clearing the debris took over nine months as recovery workers checked and rechecked for victims' remains amid tons of steel and concrete. On May 30, 2002, debris recovery was officially completed, and a somber ceremony including the removal of the last steel column marked this occasion. During 2006 and 2007, as rebuilding construction increased, human remains were found in several underground locations and atop nearby buildings, spurring yet more new searches of the area for recoverable and possibly identifiable remains. As of May 2007, 2,750 death certificates had been issued including those for victims who died on 9/11 at the WTC as well as rescue and recovery workers who died from conditions resulting from their work at the site.

Since September 2001 the repercussions of the 9/11 attacks have affected millions on a global scale, resulting in even more victims of violence to be memorialized. The "War on Terrorism" began in earnest, starting with the almost immediate invasion of Afghanistan by the United States in October 2001. The second war in Iraq began in March 2003—as of 2010, the death toll for coalition troops is almost 5,000, and civilian deaths are estimated to be in the hundreds of thousands. Other terrorist attacks by Islamic extremists have since occurred outside the United States, killing a total of 452 persons and injuring over 3,000 in the March 11, 2004, train bombings in Madrid; the July 7, 2005, bombing of trains and a bus in London; and the July 11, 2006, bombing of trains in Mumbai. Commemorative sites have been established in Madrid, London, and at the Pentagon, with the Shanksville 9/11 memorial under construction. At the WTC site proper, a complex combination of politics, economics, shifting plans for rebuilding, contests over commemoration, and reconstruction have been in process since the attacks.

Informal, "makeshift" memorials emerged in public spaces around New York City, and talk of a permanent memorial and replacing the lost buildings began immediately following the attacks. Owing to the complexity of the WTC land ownership, building ownership, existing lease contracts, and the need for both a memorial and office buildings, Governor George Pataki formed the Lower Manhattan Development Corporation (LMDC) in December 2001. The LMDC, overseen by New York State's economic development agency, has been overseeing the planning process, choosing Daniel Libeskind's Memory Foundations in 2003 as the WTC site's master rebuilding plan. Libeskind's plan included five office towers, a transit hub, retail space, a cultural center, a memorial museum, and a memorial landscape. In January 2004 Michael Arad and Peter Walker's Reflecting Absence design was chosen for the memorial landscape to be included in the master plan.[3] Processes of both planning and rebuilding have been extremely controversial, generating a number of detailed works (for example, Beauregard 2004; Rosenthal 2004; Sorkin 2003; Sturken 2004; Young 2006) outlining and critically evaluating these processes, tensions, and controversies.

CURRENT STATE OF THE WTC SITE

At the time of this writing, the National September 11 Memorial is slated for completion in September 2011, the 10-year anniversary of the attacks. The reconstruction of the area has been fraught with controversy, competing claims for space, the dislocation of businesses and people, and skyrocketing costs.[4] The site is a place where thousands of people died on 9/11, effectively becoming a graveyard endowed with a high level of contested symbolism. Construction on replacements for the major buildings that were destroyed has seemed to move at an interminably slow pace, slowed even further by constant changes in designs and alterations in building locations. Although not a part of Daniel Libeskind's Memory Foundations design for the WTC rebuilding, the first replacement building to be completed was 7 WTC, begun in 2002 and finished in 2006 at a cost of 700 million dollars. Indeed, much of Libeskind's design has been changed, including the redesign of One World Trade Center, more commonly known as Freedom Tower, by David Childs.

The commemorative cornerstone[5] for Freedom Tower was laid on July 4, 2004, only to be removed on June 22, 2006. When the original design and location were heavily altered to address security issues, the cornerstone no longer fell within the tower's planned footprint, and it was removed with far less fanfare than occurred during its installation and dedication. In December 2006 installation of the foundation beams for Freedom Tower began with two of the columns ceremonially signed by victims' family members and Libeskind. Ground was officially broken in March 2006 for Arad and Walker's commemorative landscape and for the National September 11 Memorial Museum, designed by the firm Snøhetta. While research for this book was being done, construction waxed and waned across the site; informal and formal (both temporary and permanent) memorial landscape elements were established at and close to the site, resulting in shifting loci for commemoration across parts of the site's perimeter and surrounding area over the years.

During 2001, after access to the area was available to the public, and for much of 2002, a locus for commemorative activity was at St. Paul's chapel, located east of the WTC site but far enough from the debris-recovery process during this time to be accessible along Broadway Street. In December 2001, at the WTC site itself, a public viewing platform surrounded by plywood walls opened; this became a second locus for memorialization, as the plywood walls were quickly covered with commemorative assemblages of memorial posters, flowers, candles, messages, and other commemorative offerings. The platform was closed in the summer of 2002, and in the fall a memorial fence was erected along the west side of Church Street, overlooking what was sometimes called "The Pit" (Figure 1.2). This fence, officially called a "viewing wall" by the LMDC (evoking "The Wall," the common shorthand name for the Vietnam Veterans Memorial in Washington, D.C.) opened to victims' family members and other invited guests on September 11, 2001, and to the public on September 15, 2002. The wall lined the WTC site along Church Street and part of Liberty Street and was embellished with large plaques containing listings of victims' names and a photographic and textual history of the WTC and the attacks of 9/11 in New York, Washington, D.C., and Pennsylvania. In 2004 the wall contents included the rebuilding plans for the site and over time contained other temporary visual installations. The temporary WTC Port Authority Trans-Hudson (PATH) transit station, a main hub for

26

commuters from New Jersey, reopened in 2003, and access to the station has moved multiple times as construction has progressed. In 2007 the area outside the PATH station area became one of the primary loci for commemorative activities, since construction limited pedestrian access on the remainder of the site along Church Street. The entry has now been moved again, because the station is scheduled to be replaced with a much larger transit hub designed by architect Santiago Calatrava.

The Tribute Center, an interim memorial museum, opened in September 2006 on Liberty Street along the southeast edge of the site. The Tribute Center contains a memorial exhibit and offers guided tours of the WTC site. Victims' family members work as many of the guides. And beyond the site proper, Fritz Koenig's sculpture "The Sphere," recovered from the WTC debris, was installed in Battery Park on March 11, 2002 (the six-month anniversary of the attacks), as the first truly permanent commemorative installation in Manhattan. "The Sphere," complete with

Figure 1.2 WTC site in 2005, looking west from the Millennium Hotel (© Joy Sather-Wagstaff 2005)

an eternal flame placed next to a historical marker, is located along the main thoroughfare that takes tourists to Clinton Castle and the Statue of Liberty/Ellis Island ferry dock. The area surrounding the installation is lined with park benches where locals and tourists alike eat lunch, meet friends, and relax. In the summer of 2006 the official Fire Department of New York (FDNY) Memorial Wall opened at the FDNY Engine 10 Ladder 10 station at the corner of Liberty and Greenwich, south of the WTC, and this site, along with the Tribute Center and recently opened 9/11 Memorial Preview Site at Church and Vesey Streets, constitutes the current central commemorative location. In addition, from 2002 and into the present, numerous local museums and organization have hosted 9/11 exhibits with varied foci ranging from photographs and debris to artwork and videos. These various sites make up the shifting 9/11 memoryscape in New York City and form the landscape of my Manhattan research fieldsite.

DEFINITIONS

Several of the terms used frequently in this work have multiple and contested meanings. Much of this variation is due to the different ways in which scholars across disciplines have, or have not, agreed on specific usage; in other cases differing uses of the same words depend on particular theoretical positions. The following brief sections provide specific definitions and usage justifications of my terminology.

Tourist and *Visitor*

Defining who is and who is not a tourist has been an ongoing dilemma for tourism scholars. Following the basic definitions used by the World Tourism Organization, I use the term *tourist* to describe people who are traveling away from their everyday environment and residence in order to pursue leisure activities. I also include those who are not from the region, who are visiting primarily for business activities but are also pursuing leisure activities such as visiting museums and historical sites, shopping, and theater-going. As some definitions do, I include an overnight stay (one at minimum) in my use of the term; however, I also include day-trip excursionists visiting from just beyond Manhattan who are within driving, public transport, or train distance and who are engaging in various leisure activities. This is particularly relevant in terms of Manhattan, since the Alliance for Downtown New York (ADNY 2003b:21)[6] utilizes four categories of visitors[7] for collecting tourism data that include such day-trip travelers. The ADNY categories are

Category 1: visitors from outside Lower Manhattan but within the borough of Manhattan;

Category 2: those from metro New York City suburbs, other boroughs, New York State, and mid-Atlantic states within day-travel range by car or public transportation;

Category 3: visitors from the parts of the United States beyond categories 1 and 2;

Category 4: international visitors.

I use the term *visitor* when broadly including all persons visiting a particular site or event, be they locals or non-locals.

World Trade Center versus *Ground Zero*

Some people find the use of *Ground Zero* as a name for the site in Lower Manhattan to be problematic for a wide variety of reasons. Such reasons range from an uneasy comparison to Hiroshima, the original Ground Zero of nuclear atrocity and mass death, to a dislike of or resistance to "branding" the site by the use of capital letters. "Ground Zero" is frequently used in television and print media, but *The New York Times* typically denotes the term with lowercase letters, not as a proper noun. Visitor information brochures, street signs, and kiosk maps around Manhattan identify the space as the "Former Site of the World Trade Center" or "World Trade Center" instead of using any form of "ground zero." I thus utilize the term *WTC* in respectful recognition of this as the preferred terminology in the discourses of the majority of the local New Yorkers that I met. It denotes here the precise geographical space where the twin towers and other WTC buildings once stood and where the rebuilding effort includes the cultural, business, and commemorative landscape that will, in the future, continue to be a tourist destination. In addition, the site retains and will continue to retain after rebuilding completion the name World Trade Center.

Production, Consumption, and Construction of Place

The *social production of place* is the "historical emergence and political/economic formation" of a specific material environment, whereas the *social construction and consumption of place* is the process of imbuing meanings to a site through individuals' use, memories, and images of that environment (Low 2000:127–28). *Site production* includes the process of planning, developing, and physically constructing a formal commemorative place, be it a memorial landscape, the installation of a monument, or the establishment of a museum. Participants in site production are typically various civil associations, secular or religious institutions, local and/or national government, victims' family organizations, curators and heritage management professionals, and corporate entities—and site production is the most commonly investigated aspect of commemorative, heritage, and historical sites.[8]

The *social consumption* of sites/sights encompasses the various ways in which the broader public engages with such places through experiential encounters with them and all they have to offer through sight, smell, feeling, hearing. The consumption of places also occurs through literal acts of "taking," such as photography or the purchase of objects, as well as "giving," including leaving physical traces of self at the site. The social construction of sites/sights entails the ways in which people remember their experiences and produce ongoing discourses about the place-based experience, thus constructing place meanings. Attention to the social construction and consumption of sites/sight engenders a rich understanding of how the public is critical to the creation of a wide and complex matrix of place meanings and importance that is processually constructed over time.

Performance and Performativity

Performance is understood here as the continual making and articulation of identities, selves, and meaning through stylized, embodied, variable, and repeated human acts in the everyday (Butler 1990). Performance is how we transmit knowledge to both others and ourselves in cultural practice. From speech act theory, *performance* is where the "issuing of the utterance is the performing of an action," with spoken language understood to have powerful effects in and on the social world (Austin 1975 [1962]:6). To say that something is performative is to claim that it must be enacted through performance to have both meaning and existence in the world—it is not inherently meaningful or abstractly existent. I regard places as performative. As such, embodied human activities (performances) in and of places *is* the very process of (re)making and (re)articulating place meanings over time and in space. These performances include but are not limited to polysensory engagement with the ephemeral and material culture of sites, taking photographs, crafting and telling stories about experiences, and using material and visual culture such as photographs or souvenirs for memory work.

METHODS

This work centers on fleeting human activity, visual culture, ephemeral and robust material culture, and lived experience in time and space. Therefore, I wish to highlight the ethnographic component to this research. Methods from visual anthropology in particular, as "an inquiry into all that humans make for others to see—their facial expressions, costumes, symbolic uses of space . . . as well as the full range of pictorial artifacts they produce" (Ruby 2000:ix), provided a useful framework for ethnographic engagement with tourists and their experiences with visual and material culture. Attention to visual and material culture allowed for entrance into the "multilayered, imaginative and expressive environments" (Murdock and Pink 2005:149)[9] generated by a public who actively make and use visual media, and photography was central to this process. In keeping with the most traditional use of photography as an ethnographic method, I produced a photographic record of the WTC consisting of almost 5,000 digital photographs; this record constitutes a set of ethnographic fieldnotes in addition to my written notes, maps, and audio recordings. As with written notes, photographs were dated, time stamped, and keyword coded for information such as location, specific material items in the landscape, person identification and informed consent, activities, and behaviors, all of which were used in analyses. Many of these photographs document visitors' activities while they were taking photographs of their traveling companions and objects of interest at sites and while engaging with the diverse features in commemorative landscapes and museums, generating a visual record of a wide range of data. These photos are also used as a form of illustration and narrative in and of themselves (Edwards 1997:53, 57). Selected images appear throughout the following chapters as illustrations to accompany specific textual descriptions and analyses.

My role as a photographer was also a critical form of participation observation as a means of encountering and engaging with tourists. Despite the vast number of photographs I produced, they captured only brief moments in time and are therefore very partial, incomplete documents of tourists' activities and experiences. They reveal very little about the subjective identities of these tourists and tell me nothing of what they were thinking and feeling or of the individual contexts of knowledge that shaped their travel experiences. I therefore utilized my position as a photographer as a means for initiating direct engagement with tourists at the site. As a camera-toting "fellow tourist," I was often engaged in questions or conversations about the WTC site, often when I was in the process of taking photos; this also occurred at other sites in Manhattan, Oklahoma City, and Washington, D.C. I was also frequently asked to take a photo of a group or individuals, using the cameras that they carried. After answering questions or taking these photos, I took the opportunity to introduce myself as an anthropologist studying travel to historical commemorative sites.

In some cases, I engaged in longer informal conversations with visitors on the spot or in a nearby park, café, or bench, where we could sit down. These opportunities resulted in 536 written or recorded conversations of 15 minutes to over an hour, primarily with domestic tourists from the United States but also with small samples of international visitors. This number represents only those tourists with whom I had interactions that qualified as more than very brief conversations in passing (although even the briefest conversations were rich with data). At the end of some of the longer interactions in New York, I asked tourists if they were willing to continue participating in my research after their visits by self-administering a questionnaire.[10] At the WTC site and throughout Manhattan I also performed numerous formal interviews with tourists and locals and had many informal conversations with locals.[11] Every U.S. state was represented among the domestic tourists who participated in this study; the majority were white, with a small number of African American and Latino/a tourists represented. Very few participants were Asian American and Native American. Participants were restricted to adults ages 18 and older, and they represented a wide array of occupations, from university students, homemakers, and professionals to skilled workers, schoolteachers, and retirees. International tourists in the study came from Argentina, Bosnia, Canada, China, Colombia, Ecuador, Germany, Ghana, India, Italy, Japan, South Korea, Mexico, Pakistan, Spain, and the United Kingdom.

Given claims that tourists are highly reluctant to give up their travel time to talk to researchers, I was at first surprised by the willingness of these tourists to take the time to speak with me at length. I attribute part of this willingness to my being perceived as nonthreatening—in general, female journalists, protestors, and other nontourists at sites had far more success than did males in approaching and speaking with both tourists and local visitors. However, the fact that these commemorative spaces were considered by visitors to be important historical sites representative of events that affected them in many highly personal ways bears more forcefully on their enthusiastic responses. They deeply desired to tell their stories and share their experiences, particularly to someone who would be sharing them with an audience outside their everyday communities of belonging.

Our encounters with one another revealed the highly complex, diverse, and personalized ways in which tourists experienced commemorative sites. The narratives that tourists constructed and performed—immediate responses to the sites, stories of their experiences, and their representations and displays of selves and experiences—are central to my understanding of how tourists engage with and mark and make commemorative sites through the embodied consumption and performance of visual and material culture. Such complex and diverse information cannot be derived through analyses of visual or textual media or through observation alone; it requires the ethnographic intimacy of actually engaging with people who are in the thick of lived experiences. This ethnographic intimacy was also critical to understanding the WTC site as a highly contested place, a site whose meanings are diverse and in constant flux despite the ongoing establishment of official textual, photographic, and architectural narratives of commemoration in the landscape.

These research strategies were highly productive for generating a rich analysis of the various ways in which tourists and tourism play a role in the marking and making of contemporary commemorative sites.

OUTLINE OF THE BOOK

The social construction of memory, historicity, and commemorative sites through various social practices of tourism is the key focus of this book; this phenomenon is framed within a broad selection of existing social sciences and humanities literature on memory, history, space and place, and tourism. Chapter 2 contains a review and critique of a cross-disciplinary selection of this literature, identifying key strengths and weaknesses, core concepts and frameworks, and lacunae in empirical evidence that preclude more complex understandings of these topics. At issue is a negotiation of the intersections between theory and methods in terms of making tourists and others who engage with commemorative landscapes and their lived subjective experiences the focus of study rather than just commemorative objects and landscapes.

Chapter 3 presents a critical overview of academic theories and popular perspectives on "dark tourism" (Lennon and Foley 2000:1). Both academic and popular perspectives view visitation to "dark" sites such as the WTC primarily as a response to the lure of death and disaster and only secondarily as a form of pilgrimage or commemoration. Journalist John Hill (2006) writes that

> of the various elements that comprise [sic] the rebuilding effort at Ground Zero, the one that will attract the most visitors is most surely Arad's memorial. Here we pass from the world of architourism into that of "tragic tourism," where people are drawn to Civil War battlefields, concentration camps, terrorist sites, and places of destruction and loss. From the very first cries of "rebuild!"—predating any master plan or building designs—one consideration has been the huge number of visitors that will visit the site, an acknowledgment of its obvious importance but also of the magnetism of tragedy.[12]

Dark tourism, John Lennon and Malcom Foley's (2000) term for this "tragic tourism," has become increasingly mainstreamed beyond the academy in the years since 9/11. The 2007 edition of Lonely Planet's *Best in Travel* bluelist includes the first official feature on dark tourism, discussing sites of celebrity death, disaster-aid travel, and historical sites such as the Killing Fields of Cambodia. The term has entered mainstream journalistic media and is used to describe tourism to 9/11 sites such as the World Trade Center and Shanksville, Pennsylvania; New Orleans as it continues to recover from the 2005 devastation wrought by Hurricane Katrina; Indonesia after the 2004 tsunami; and Southeast China and Haiti following the earthquakes of 2008 and 2010. I discuss the theoretical and methodological limitations that this relatively new intellectual and scholarly concept of dark tourism places on our current and future understanding of tourism to commemorative historical sites as socially constructive.

Chapter 4 explores how and why tourism, historical site production, and consumption are frequently framed by scholars and cultural critics as a Disneyfication and commodification of tragedy, an erasure of "real history" and a profaning of the dead. In such frameworks, the consumption of commodities is understood to be meaningless, inauthentic, or socially destructive; in the case of the WTC, such a position engenders a fear that the site is not now and will fail to become a properly sanctified historical and commemorative site. I deconstruct some of the assumptions that underlie this criticism of consumption and commodities as socially unconstructive, arguing that these assumptions explicitly and implicitly inform many of the anxieties over the relationships between tourism, commemoration, heritage, and historicity. In contrast, understanding consumption as a culturally productive and constructive act engenders insight into how certain forms of consumption can work "to negate the abstract nature of the commodity through rituals of appropriation by which social groups [and thus identities] are created" (Miller 1993:19) and reproduced. People and places are both argued to be made—socially constructed—through performative, culturally meaningful acts of consumption such as tourism.

I consider tourism, as a form of constructive consumption, to play a key role in grappling with a "heritage that hurts," given that it is through visitation to commemorative sites that some of the most powerful physical and emotional engagement with the visual and material culture of tragic events occurs. It is also through this engagement and the various tourist practices that are performed both on-site and post-visit that the diverse and dominant meanings accorded to memorial sites and the events and victims commemorated are socially constructed over time. I thus posit that tourists should be understood as participating agents in the social production, consumption, performance, and construction of historically salient commemorative sites through various tourist and everyday practices, both during travel and post-travel. Chapters 5–7 address a selection of these on- and off-site practices.

Chapter 5 presents ethnographic data on the performative activities that mark visitors' presence in commemorative memoryscapes, including graffiti and other forms that literally mark the site, the making of commemorative folk assemblages, the purchase of souvenirs, and taking photographs. These creative practices are contemporary correlates to the "Memorial Impulse" (Sloane 1991:165)[13] that has influenced monumental architecture and individual sentimentality since the late 19th century while also marking a late 20th-century reemergence of a Western public culture of mourning in a time when death has been fully privatized by our own medical system and funeral industry. These various acts of *marking* places and presence are, I argue, a central part of the process of *making* places historically salient and meaningful both individually and collectively, given that they persist in memory and material form far beyond the performance of the acts themselves. Chapter 6 attends to a number of issues with museums and memorials as places of collection—of both the material and visual culture of tragedy and of the public—that are for recollecting memories and constructing historicity. I discuss the creation of popular symbolic architectural elements and "official" commemorative narratives, the ethics and politics of display, and the diverse ways in which people personalize these sites and the events that they commemorate while engaging with the material and visual culture of tragedy and for memory. The sites under discussion include the WTC site in the present and as planned for the future, the Oklahoma City National Memorial, the Vietnam Veterans Memorial, the United States Holocaust Memorial Museum, the Pentagon memorial, the Madrid M11 memorial, and the future Flight 93 memorial landscape.

The ways in which the collectible and documentary material culture of travel—such as photographs and souvenirs—accompanies, embellishes, or provokes performative narratives and serves as tacit physical evidence of sites seen and experienced is presented in Chapter 7. Such narratives and material culture play performative roles in processually constructing and maintaining memories of travel and thus site meanings within changing social and political post-visit contexts. As a result of off-site research, I present the private and semiprivate cultures of circulation that encompass tourist photographs, souvenirs bought, scrapbooks created, and travel narratives told as they intersect with and influence broader public memory-making and historicity. These cultures of collection and circulation also have a creative and museological sensibility as tourists see themselves as personal historians who document and display everyday, intimate life with family, friends, and numerous communities of belonging. My post-visit examination of material and visual culture reveals that consumptive and performative culture does significant social labor in building identities and memories and by extension, in the ongoing social construction of places seen and experienced over time and across space.

CHAPTER 2

Memory, Space/Place, Tourism: Paradigms and Problems

Figure 2.1 Item left by a visitor on the WTC viewing wall
(© Joy Sather-Wagstaff 2004)

HISTORY, HISTORICITY, AND MEMORY

From Holocaust death camp sites and museums, Cambodia's Killing Fields, and Ghana's Elmina slave castle to Civil War battlefields in Gettysburg and the Oklahoma City National

Memorial, historical sites commemorating the victims of some of humanity's darkest hours exist around the world. Since the turn of the 21st century, commemorative sites have continued to emerge as human acts of violence persist and natural disasters of scale occur. Such sites also include the former location of the WTC's twin towers in New York City, Madrid's M11 memorial in Spain, the Kigali Memorial Center in Rwanda, Hurricane Katrina memorials in New Orleans and Biloxi, and Indonesia's Aceh Tsunami Museum. As historical places for memory and historical consciousness, these commemorative sites play key roles in the construction and maintenance of nationalism, national or ethnic identities, lessons-to-be-learned, and political ideologies. Tourism is one of the main means for experiential encounters with commemorative sites, and it also generates a set of practices that mark and make such sites as meaningful and historically salient for both individuals and broader communities of belonging. Understanding this process requires a serious consideration of the interconnected roles that experientiality, along with material and visual culture, plays in the social construction of memory, historicity, place-making, and tourism itself.

Memory, both collective and individual, is and has been an enduring topic of scholarly interest in the social sciences and humanities. In the last decades of the 20th century and into the present, attention to the processes and politics of history, historical consciousness, and memory by scholars in anthropology and numerous other human-centered disciplines has increased at a rapid pace.[1] It is on this recent work that I focus here. In particular I wish to challenge the ongoing tendency to distinguish history, historical consciousness, and memory as clearly separable cultural phenomena, structuring history as "dominant, official narratives" in high contrast to memory and historical consciousness as "vernacular, individual narratives" of what has happened in the past.[2] This oppositional structuring is perhaps most clear in Pierre Nora's conceptualization of history versus memory, in which "history is perpetually suspicious of memory, and its true mission is to destroy it" (1989:9). It is also, in part, a reflection of utilizing Foucauldian understandings of social knowledge hierarchies, in which memory is understood to be one form of the "subjugated knowledges" that are largely unrecognized by institutions or are counter to official discourses and thus represent cultural resistance to dominant narratives (Foucault 1980:82).

Drawing from works that build constructively on these positions while questioning the validity of such cleanly oppositional formulations, the conceptual framework for this book considers history, historicity, and memory as inseparable and mutually constituting and attends to the experiential as central to the social processes of knowledge construction about the past in the present. *Historicity* is defined here as the "culturally patterned way or ways of experiencing and understanding history" (Ohnuki-Tierney 1990:4), and it shapes and is shaped by our identities, "the names we give to the different ways in which we are positioned by, and position ourselves within, the narratives of the past" (Hall 1990:225). I prefer the term *historicity* to that of *historical consciousness* for the same reasons as Emiko Ohnuki-Tierney does: to "avoid the inference that how people think and experience history is always conscious" (1990:4, fn. 4). Historicity is understood to be dynamic and complex, not static and uncomplicated, and although collective historicities and histories may appear monolithic and heterogenous, individuals' historicities and histories can be quite diverse. Individual and collective historicities are also mutually constitutive, inseparable, and enacted through various dialogic, discursive strategies. The formation of historicities requires the "active involvement of historical actors—they use, select, and create their own understanding of history as they act upon the collective notion of historicity" (Ohnuki-Tierney 1990:20).

Michel-Rolph Trouillot likewise identifies the inseparability of history and historicity as well as how both result from the same set of selective processes. For Trouillot both history and historicity are "the facts of the matter and a narrative of those facts, both 'what happened' and 'that which is said to have happened'" (1995:2). The "facts of the matter" refer to the actual sociohistorical process, whereas "narrative" emphasizes the heavily mediated social knowledge of that process. Trouillot draws our attention to the silencing of other narratives and (subjugated) knowledge in the power-laden creation of "official" representations of the past—"History." Such representations are highly selective; they serve to maintain the interests of the elite or otherwise powerful who produce them, and they are codified in various forms, most often written but also very importantly through the public display of national patrimony in landscapes and museums (Handler and Gable 1997; White 2004; Zolberg 1998). This particular characterization of "History" delineates such knowledge as in opposition to other forms of knowledge (for example, memory) about the past, albeit somewhat necessarily for the sake of delineating the power deployed in the social construction of said knowledge.

In discussing the making of memory and history from a different side of the power imbalance, Darlene Clark Hine introduces the notion of "cultural dissemblage," the creation of protective appearances of truthfulness about and full disclosure of past events to describe the self-silencing, partial narratives of African American women (1994:37). History, historicity, and memory are often taken to be cultural assemblages or "complete collections." Yet given that these collections are highly selective, they change over time and are thus not necessarily comprehensive as a whole totality of all gained knowledge, and they are subject to ever-changing interpretive and temporal contexts, they may better be more effectively understood as both assemblage and dissemblage: "(diss)assemblages." Events and experiences are not only selectively remembered (or forgotten) but may also perhaps even be selectively forgotten (or remembered) at a later date, under differing circumstances, and for very different ends. Thus history, historicity, and memory are all created with a high level of selectivity, a construction that is also under constant deconstruction and reconstruction.

And historicity is thus inseparably intertwined with both memory and history; these are all part and parcel of the same social processes of coming to know about the past, crafting and re-crafting cultural (diss)assemblages over time. Historicities and memories are also histories in their own right, not completely separate from or always necessarily in opposition to a given official "History."

Although "history" in the most canonical, academic sense is typically some form of institutionally sanctioned, historiographic narrative, members of the broad public do consider themselves to also be "history-makers." They see themselves as personal historiographers in the everyday, creating individual and collective narratives that include both their past experiences and those gleaned from broader "Histories" and the experiences of others. Memory and historicity constitute these personal and collective histories. The artificial boundaries we often set between "History," histories, historicity, and memory are thus actually highly permeable in vernacular, everyday practices.

Historicity is indeed constituted by retained (but not necessarily recalled in the performative, enacted sense) cultural knowledge—memories—about past events and experiences. It is a (diss)assemblage, a selective and ongoing diss-assemblage and re-assemblage of knowledge taken from an array of sources including external sources, such as official historical narratives or others' individual recollections and/or from one's own memories of actually experiencing events. The construction of this knowledge does not necessarily require being a first-hand witness to or participant in an event and its aftermath as it unfolds in time and space but does require some form of "second-hand" witnessing to such. Second-hand witnessing may include the consumption of visual and textual media forms (television and print media, photographs, or film), hearing oral narratives of events, or encounters with material and visual culture in museums or at historical sites. And witnessing in and of itself, be it first or second hand, implicitly requires bodily engagement in some form or forms, from seeing and touching to hearing and even smelling.

The politics and practices of witnessing are central in much of the scholarly literature on representations of Holocaust history in terms of photography, the built environment, and the display of material artifacts at such sites as museums, memorial landscapes, and the death camps. It is, to date, the most comprehensive literature on commemorative historical sites that we have to draw from when performing research on and at similar, yet very distinct commemorative sites. In terms of understanding the potential of the experiential for memory and historicity-making through travel to commemorative sites, the works of James Young (1993) and Alison Landsberg (1997, 2004) are particularly valuable. Young explores the tactile and visual aspects of Holocaust memorial landscapes and museums, what he terms "the texture of memory," that which is created for bodily encounter as a means for "memory-telling" (1993:ix). He provides a cogent explanation of such sites as anything but static representations of the past in that through multiple levels of interpretation they "speak" differentially to individuals owing to changing temporal contexts and differing subjectivities. And, like Young, Andreas Huyssen calls our attention to how "memory and forgetting pervade real public space" in contemporary life as memorial landscapes, monuments, and other public spaces of commemoration increasingly appear in our cities, making physical encounters with places for public memory unavoidable (2003:9).

Landsberg (2004:2) introduces the provocative, powerful, and very useful notion of "prosthetic memory," a form of memory that "emerges at the interface between a person and a historical narrative about the past, at an experiential site such as a movie theater or museum" or, I add, a commemorative landscape or when viewing travel photographs. She argues that this is a newer form of memory, one that is a result of mass cultural technologies of reproduction such as film and photography and that it has the potential to transform memory and identity politics by generating empathic understandings of others' historical experiences and first-hand witnessing.[3] Yet as will be discussed further in Chapter 3, some forms of historical representation are considered by scholars to be more "authentic" than others and thus "better" representations of the past, and they reject representations that derive from contemporary technologies of reproduction as inauthentic "edutainment." One example of this is from film historian Thomas Elsaesser (1996), who posits that experiential memory-making has negative consequences, contributing to the over-production of cultural obsessions with trauma and empty rituals of spectatorship and storytelling.

Scholarly works on the Holocaust as well as other tragedies of scale also draw our attention sharply to the critical issue of contestation: whose memories and what versions of historical events are represented? Contestation is indeed a part of the construction of historicity and memory, yet it is often represented through the binary terms, whereby official "History" is something that memory (individual and collective) contests in a dialectical tug-of-war. Some scholars often call this contestational memory "cultural memory" (Sturken 1997; Taylor 2005), blurring the lines between individual and collective memory and maintaining the opposition between "official" and "vernacular" knowledge of the past. I find that this is sometimes an effective framework, but it unfortunately tends to subsume localized or individual knowledge into a too broad realm of "collective knowledge." In contrast, Bodnar proposes a triadic, dialogic model for the cultural knowledge and expressions we call history, historicity, and memory: "official," "public," and "vernacular" (1992:13–15). Given that my research focuses on the activities and experiences of tourists, an ordinary public, as they engage with "official" and "public" realms of knowledge, Bodnar's triad is a very useful framework for tracing the relationships between different yet intertwined memorywork modes in everyday practice.

Bodnar applies his triadic model for historiography, whereas I adapt it for ethnographic research with a living, agentic public. The participants in my research, both locals and non-locals, represent the vernacular (multiple, local, individual, and heterogeneous) aspect of the triad. Public history and memory are that which is constructed through these individuals' engagement with official historicization in the context of their own specific memories and historicities. Official historicization is that which is produced through the establishment of codified narratives of events and formal commemorative landscapes as well as official ceremonies and museological practices. Official, public, and vernacular history and memory are argued here to constitute one another in various diverse and sometimes contestational ways, and thus tracing these relationships is critical to understanding the highly complex making of a commemorative historical site. By attending to these relationships, I aim to engender a richer under-standing of how such sites are processually made into places for diverse memories and histories by all involved parties, both at and beyond the site proper, rather than simply being officially produced by institutions and then passively consumed by the public.

CULTURAL SITES: MAKING SPACES/PLACES FOR MEMORY AND HISTORY

Memory and history are sometimes mistakenly understood as "things" inscribed on, encoded in, or contained within material objects in the built or natural environment, such as ruins, mon-uments, houses, mountains, boulders, or vegetation (Küchler 1993), and this reification is particularly true of commemorative sites. Historian John Gillis (1994) criticizes such reification of memory, history, and identity as material objects in space (and by extension, as "contained" within or inscribed on them) and urges us to look instead at how engagement with material objects in space and over time play a role in the processual mediation and performance of memory. Nora (1989) likewise notes that memory relies heavily on material traces, yet memory itself is not imbed-ded in or on material things. Moving away from a position that deems memory and history to be naturally auto-encoded on the landscape or in objects and toward one that attends to the social processes of remembrance that involve materiality engenders an understanding of the highly complex social and political economy and machinery of memory and history-making (Küchler 1993).

One way to to understand the social processes of remembrance without further reifying and objectifying "memory" and "his-tory" is to shift linguistically to a more performative description of place-making and places themselves. Academic and popular discourses alike use the word "of" when articulating the rela-tionships between space/place, memory, history, historicity, and identity (Küchler 1993), marking places as somehow containing memory rather than working in the service of making memory. The Vietnam Veterans Memorial in Washington, D.C., is referred to as "a place of memory" in academic literature, throughout tourist brochures, in the popular media, and in the talk of visitors at the site. Similarly, Edward Linenthal describes remnant building footprints and traces of ghetto walls in Eastern Europe as "places of memory," both of the events of the Holocaust and of pre-Holocaust Jewish life (1995, 2001). If we are to understand places and memory both to be truly processual, as Henri Lefebvre (1991 [1974]) asserts them to be, then I propose that we should treat and speak of such sites as places *for* making memory and history, rather than *of* memory and history.

Sites of historical and cultural importance that represent violent events are particularly prone to a social misunderstanding about their emergence; it is believed that they have come into existence only through the events that take place at a particular location: wars result in battlefields, genocides produce mass graves, the assassination site of a political leader delineates a national sacred place. However, historical commemorative places are not "made" as important sites simply because of the events that may physically mark them as distinct places through bloodshed or the destruction of buildings or landscapes. As will be addressed, like all the sites that make up our lived and perceived sociocultural realities, these places are made through ongoing human practices in time and, I argue, across multiple spaces and places. The distinctions between space and place are key to understanding both phenomena as human-made. Yi-Fu Tuan provides the most succinct yet complex definitions for space and place, maintaining that space and place fundamentally "require each other for definition" and that

> "space" is more abstract than "place." What begins as undifferentiated space becomes place as we get to know it better and *endow it with value.* . . . Furthermore, if we think of space as that which allows movement, then place is pause; each pause in a movement makes it possible for location to be transformed into place. (Tuan 1977:6, emphasis added)

In addition, although space is more abstract than place, it is not absolutely so, because it, too, is defined by human activity.

Michel de Certeau defines space as "composed of intersections of mobile elements . . . actuated by the ensemble of movements deployed within it," and it is communicative narratives, spoken or otherwise articulated, that perform the "labor that constantly transforms places into spaces and spaces into places" (1984:117–18). Space and place are thus made by human practice—various activities and experiences—and the "stories" (narratives) of such play a fundamental role in the construction of the meanings endowed to spaces and places.

Although places are physically located at fixed coordinates, as a type of "cultural sites" they also exist in other spaces and places of cultural knowledge and practice (Hastrup and Fog Olwig 1997:4). In considering them to also be "unfixed" sites, I offer here a means to understand how commemorative places also exist—and are made—through the historicities of individuals and in the collective memories of numerous communities of belonging as performed in the everyday, not just at a commemorative site. For de Certeau, memory is "a sort of anti-museum; it is not localizable" even when it involves the evocation of a specific place (1984:108). Yet memory itself is spatialized; as Jonathan Z. Smith writes, we use the "'I can't place it' to refer to lapses of memory" (1987:26). Remembering and knowing are thus spatial practices, since knowledge about a fixed site can be evoked when I am far beyond that place through reverie, narratives, images, or texts; such evocation in turn continues to (re)construct the meanings of the place remembered. I consider this particular notion of memory and historicity as spatialized cultural sites to be a key means for understanding the multiple sites for and processes of meaning-making, a critical component to considering the roles that tourism, as a multisited set of practices, play in the making of commemorative sites.

SITE-MAKING AND TOURISM

As with all places, the making of commemorative sites occurs through the entangled, processual, and dialogic practices of social production, construction, performance, and consumption.

The social production of sites is characterized by the "historical emergence and political/economic formation" of a specific material setting (Low 2000:127–28). Given this definition, we would include in commemorative historical site production the processes of planning, developing, and physically constructing a formalized site, be it a memorial landscape, the installation of a monument, or the establishment of a museum, the selection of its contents, and the design of exhibits. Participants in commemorative site production include architects, civil associations, secular or religious groups, local and/or national government, survivors and victims' family organizations, curators and heritage management professionals, and corporate entities. This is the most predominantly researched facet of commemorative, heritage, and historical sites (for example, Foote 2001 [1997]; Gillis 1994; Linenthal 1995, 2001) and, to date, is one of the many foci for scholarly articles and books as well as mass media books on the events and aftermath of 9/11 and the WTC rebuilding process.

The social construction, performance, and consumption of sites are the transformative and socially mediated processes of creating place meanings through various social practices (Low 2000:128). These processes include the ways in which the broader public actively constructs both place meanings and subjectivities through phenomenological experiences at sites, the production of ongoing discourses about the place-based experience, and the social circulation of memories of the experience. Meaning-making is a performative process of "mobilizing and reconfiguring space and places" (Coleman and Crang 2002:10), whereby places and selves are dialogically transformed and multiple, diverse, and sometimes fragmentary meanings and memory are created and performed. As an exercise in understanding this transformational process, I focus principally on the roles that tourists, as representatives of a geographically dispersed public, play in these processes of production, construction, performance, and consumption. Acts of walking through the WTC site, seeing, feeling, listening, and even smelling in the environment, and marking it through graffiti, commemorative activities, and photography, structure many tourists' experiences and memories of their visits. These acts of memory-making, as performed post-travel through narratives and the circulation and display of the material culture of travel that then "traverse and organize" (de Certeau 1984:115) the site from a distance, are a part of the process of making places historically salient and meaningful, both individually and collectively. The historical importance and meaningfulness of commemorative sites are not simply imposed superstructurally but are constructed through actions generated by a broad public, and, as such, they are thus places that human "imagination seeks to [both] change and appropriate" (Lefebvre 1991 [1974]:33).

When at commemorative sites such as the WTC, the Oklahoma City National Memorial, or the Vietnam Veterans Memorial in Washington, D.C., tourists play a key part in the making of these places through their presence, actions, and experiences. Being there and doing actions are considered by tourists to be central to making their whole experience authentic and meaningful. The performative recollections of these actions in turn construct, in part, the experiences of other visitors and, when performed post-visit, knowledge for those who may never visit the site. However, tourists and even many local visitors are rarely acknowledged as participatory agents in this process; they are instead seen as end-point consumers whose meaning-making agency is limited to the interpretations of sites/ sights already produced by various organizations.

In his analysis of the emergence of historical sites representing violent events in the U.S. landscape and how the "stories of these sites offer insight into how people grapple with the meaning of tragedy," Kenneth Foote (2001 [1997]) offers such a production-centered framework for understanding how such sites are marked and made. According to Foote the marking and making of these sites as meaningful occur through one of four processes: sanctification, designation, rectification, or obliteration (2001 [1997]:7). The process of sanctification best describes the process at the WTC site (as well as other 9/11 event sites) and other commemorative sites such as the Oklahoma City National Memorial, the John Lennon Strawberry Fields memorial in Central Park, the Columbine High School memorial, Gettysburg, and Dealey Plaza, the site of President John F. Kennedy's assassination.

Sanctification involves the physical creation of a specific place that represents a loss to a broad public rather than single individuals; it is ritually made distinct by the emplacement and maintenance of a "durable marker" of scale such as a memorial garden or park landscape, monument, or building (Foote 2001 [1997]:8–15). A space is thus marked and made to be sacred in a secular (rather than religious) sense of veneration and consecration. Although Foote provides this most useful definition for commemorative and historical sites of scale and presents a thorough discussion on the governmental and civic organizations that bring about their physical existence in the landscape, he fails to account for any part of their actual consumption and construction by a broader public. Likewise, he pays little attention to the memorial museum institutions that accompany many commemorative landscapes, such as in Oklahoma City and as planned for the WTC site and the United States Holocaust Memorial Museum, and that serve as memorial sites despite being geographically distant from the sites of tragic events. These, too, are sites for consumption by a broad public.

Given that many of these visitors from the broader public are tourists, then tourists (and tourism) must be considered as a significant part of the broader social making of commemorative places, both landscapes and museums. Tourists represent the widest public for whom the sites are intended to serve and who, through visitation, actively engage with these commemorative memoryscapes, making the material culture of memory (such as photographs) and generating individual and collective memory historicity through such practices. They are not simply consuming the official narratives of memorial landscapes but engaging their own subjectivities in dialog with such narratives, constructing a wide array of site meaningfulness. And despite a tendency among scholars, heritage practitioners, and the general public to think of formalized landscapes and memorial museums as already "made," these landscapes and museums are, in actual sociocultural practice, continually made and remade through visitation and active interpretation by tourists. There is indeed an ongoing contest of meaning that links the social production of commemorative sites with the social construction engendered by the visitors who consume these memoryscapes.

Commemorative sites are tourist destinations for a number of reasons; most generally they form one dimension of what tourism scholars denote as historical, heritage, or cultural tourism. David Chidester and Edward Linenthal suggest that commemorative sites are "intimately entangled in such 'profane' enterprises as tourism, economic exchange, and development" (1995:1), but public and scholarly discourse generally fails to explicitly acknowledge tourists' practices as playing any significant roles in the development and maintenance of historically salient commemorative sites. As a commemorative place in process, the WTC site provided a unique opportunity for ethnographic research into the social production, consumption, performance, and construction of a memorial place in transition from an informal to a formal commemorative site. My work at and beyond the WTC is thus a contribution to research on commemorative sites given that currently, in-depth scholarly works have been largely limited temporally to international war and Holocaust sites/ sights, concentrated on memorial objects (museum artifacts/ exhibits and monumental architecture), or focused on the production of various sites by organizations rather than their social construction by a broader public, typically tourists. Yet tourists can, for many scholarly and practicing researchers, be troublesome subjects for study.

THE TROUBLE WITH TOURISTS I: SUBJECTS, SITING, METHODS

I view tourism as a set of sociocultural practices that are systemic and processual, a means for the cultural performance and circulation of embodied experiences, landscapes, memories, narratives, bodies, images, material culture, and identities. This ongoing cultural circulation is understood to dialogically link the public world with the private, the individual with various communities of belonging, the past with the present and future, and the local with the national and global, engendering numerous productive effects, both positive and negative. Within the specific context of tourism studies, I both engage with and challenge current paradigms and approaches. In particular, I consider the limited understanding we have of cultural and historical authenticity and the meaningfulness of leisure travel practices under (post)modernity and globalization owing to both methodological issues and canonical, scholarly constructions of tourists and tourism writ large.

Until recently, dominant approaches in tourism studies have focused almost exclusively on every possible aspect of tourism, including tourist destinations, as the primary subjects of study—except for the actual tourists. The social and cultural impacts of travel on tourists themselves and the communities of belonging in which they participate are largely missing in the tourism literature, even that from within anthropology and other social sciences. The exclusion of tourists as primary subjects derives from a canonization of particular research topics, the subjectivities and paradigms of tourism scholars, and academic discourses on who constitutes legitimate subjects of study as well as where and how they should be studied. As Sharon Gmelch (2004:8) points out, tourism research across disciplines has focused primarily on issues of origins and impacts; specifically, where people go and to a lesser extent why they travel, how and when tourism developed, how destinations are marketed, economic and environmental impacts, and the social and cultural impacts on local communities.

The seminal works of Erik Cohen and Dean MacCannell, scholars who pioneered tourism as a legitimate subject of study for social scientists beginning in the late 1960s and early 1970s, established this paradigm, and it continues to be reproduced despite the exponential growth of academic tourism research in a wide range of disciplines in the 1990s (Aramberri 2003:964).[4] In the case of works dealing specifically with "dark" tourism, tourists are largely absent from the research and the resulting literature. Of the eight essays in the volume edited by Graham Dann and Anthony Seaton, *Slavery, Contested Heritage, and Thanatourism* (2001), only three engage with human subjects in any manner, and these are not site visitors but museum curators (Seaton 2001), the owners and directors of historical plantations sites in the southern United States (Butler 2001), and tour guides (Roushanzamir and Kreshel 2001). All eight utilize tourism materials such as brochures and other promotional materials, literature reviews, novels, travel memoirs, historical documents, and some personal observations of the sites as primary sources for data. Only one essay included the voice of a solitary site visitor; in this case, cited from a published newspaper interview, not encountered by the author first hand (Eskew 2001). In some cases it was even unclear as to when or if the authors had physically visited the site and if so, for how long and under what circumstances. However, Dann and Seaton do briefly acknowledge that these case studies are one-sided in that they do not include the experiences of those who visit the site, and they call for this to be part of future research projects on similar sites (2001:24). Although research and publication have been done on human interaction and place-making at the WTC (for example, Greenspan 2006; Gutman 2009; Lisle 2004; Watts 2009), few researchers, such as filmmakers Jean Sébastien Marcoux and Renaud Legoux (2005), have explicitly engaged with tourists at the site as a central part of the research process.

The interrelated issues of methods and what or who constitute valid subject(s) for study and where and how they are to be studied remain topics rarely discussed forthrightly or in significant detail in scholarly literature on tourism.[5] To actually talk to and actively engage with tourists is a surprisingly underutilized method in tourism studies; to take them seriously as agentic subjects and describe them and theorize their experiences from their perspective is an even more novel idea.[6] Edward Bruner (1989) has argued (and continues to do so) that tourists should be able to speak for themselves in our research, yet they and their voices are still largely absent in scholarly works. Thus "much of what has been written about tourists is based only inconsistently on what tourists actually have to say about their own experiences" (Harrison 2003:39). Tourists are instead, as previously noted, usually spoken for and described using "the often disparaging remarks by certain authors, such as Daniel Boorstin, none of whom has conducted a systematic, first-hand study of these subjects" (Nash 2001:494). Tourists are not ethnographic subjects. Julia Harrison explains her frustration with how

> the repeated assertion in the literature that we really know little about what the tourist actually experiences, and why so many thousands, if not millions of Westerners and other First World citizens find travel a meaningful experience, fuelled my confusion about why many in the academy, and other critical voices, speak so disparagingly of the experience. (2003:205)

Julio Aramberri, in reviewing Harrison's book, also criticizes this tendency, asking the reader: "Is the tourist really as empty, pretentious, or vicious as our maîtres-à-penser portend him/her to be? The [tourist] character has often been convicted of everything short of parricide and good taste" (2003:964).

Frustration with this scholarly paradigm that disparages tourists and their experiences outright without making efforts to understand them from a first-hand perspective has motivated scholars such as Harrison and I to explicitly make tourists the focal subjects of and participants in our ethnographic studies. We do so as a means to move beyond assuming that we know what tourists are getting out of their travel simply by observing them and instead working with them actively, participating in activities with them and taking seriously what they say about their experiences. This approach is not intended as a method to demonstrate that tourists are all necessarily "good, nice" people or that they irrefutably and totally defy the common stereotypes that they have been assigned but is an approach that takes tourists as seriously as we do our other, more traditional ethnographic subjects. By doing this, we contribute to the small but growing body of works that aim to understand the meaningfulness of travel as a social practice.

According to Bruner this kind of ethnographic research is that which understands and analyzes tourism "not as representations, metaphors, texts, or simulacra of something located elsewhere, but a *social practice to be studied in its own right*, grounded by methods of ethnography. This is taking tourism seriously" (2005:7, emphasis added). One of the fundamental values of this approach is, as Bruner has consistently argued, an extended understanding of tourism, tourists, and their social practices as emergent, performative, and agentic. Focusing on tourists as subjects using ethnographic, qualitative methods also engenders critical and rich knowledge about the demand-side—or rather, as I present throughout this work, the construction, performance, and consumption sides—of the tourism equation. This is an approach called for by tourism scholars such as Dann and Seaton (2001), Lennon and Foley (2000), and Lawrence Mintz (2004), but it has yet to be carried out broadly in academic research owing to, at least in part, general methodological deficiencies and, within anthropology, dominant notions of what constitutes one's fieldwork and fieldsite(s).

The mechanics and logistics of studying a highly mobile population, such as tourists, are indeed contributing factors in why tourists themselves are rarely the ethnographic subjects and thus primary sources of research data. Tourists stay in places for short periods of time, and they are usually very widely dispersed once they return to their places of residency. This situation makes the sustained and intimate interactions normatively expected for ethnographic research quite difficult. How, then, do we "purposively create the occasions for contacts that might well be as mobile, diffuse, and episodic as the processes" we study, such as tourists and tourism, and "where do we 'hang out'" (Amit 2000:15) to perform our fieldwork? Notably, the issue of mobile populations is not only a problem when studying tourists but for research on any mobile, geographically diffuse individuals including, but not limited to, immigrants, seasonal workers, consultants, certain types of entrepreneurs, diaspora populations, people in transit-system occupations, and missionaries. Anthropologists, including me, who make tourists central subjects in their research do so with methods that challenge some of the disciplinary notions of how ethnographic research should be sited and performed, working creatively against the single-site, terminal collectivity norm of fieldwork. In the process of doing this, we also often blur the distinctions between "home" and "away" that traditionally and artificially delineate the realms of our everyday social and scholarly existence from those of our active research fieldwork sites.

One means of engaging directly with a tourist population for a relatively extended period of time on-site is to literally travel with a group by securing a position as a tour guide, group member, group chaperone, or even as an academic instructor for a study abroad program.[7] As part of his research on tourism and cultural performances, Bruner worked as a tour guide and academic lecturer for a group tour to Indonesia (1995) and traveled across Africa (South Africa, Zimbabwe, Botswana, Tanzania, Kenya, and Egypt) as a member in a luxury group tour (2005:13). George Gmelch (2004) investigated U.S. university students' travel practices and experiences in Europe while he was an anthropology course instructor for a study abroad trip and Rebekah Sobel, as a group leader for Birthright Israel, researched U.S. Jewish youths from Georgetown University on a group trip to Israel (2009). In my research I spent numerous days on different guided group tours of Manhattan, getting to know my fellow tourists quite well over the course of the few hours or half-day of the tour, spending time both experiencing the sites seen together and discussing them in conversations. These opportunities constitute a form of participant observation, whereby one not only observes the conditions and narratives of the guided tour or trip and how tourists interact and respond to one another and the tour but also participates as a tourist and, as such, cultivates engagement and discussions with fellow participants that result in rich narrative data. But what about when these practices are not feasible, because of either issues of monetary resources or situational access to groups traveling together for an extended period of time?

Another approach involves focusing the research project on one particular locale or a series of related sites, depending on the research questions posed. In this mode of study the site becomes as much of a focal subject as the people, both tourists and locals, who use the space in various ways. Tim Edensor (1998), researching tourism at the Taj Mahal, spent six months total at the site and around Agra over the course of four years, interacting with both locals who worked in the tourist trade (vendors and tour guides) and tourists, domestic and international. He also performed extensive historical and cultural research on the site, providing a historically deep context for understanding the diverse complexity of national, local, and tourist meanings accorded to the Taj Mahal and as they have been and continue to be constructed. Bruner (1993, 1994) explored the New Salem Historical Site, the reconstruction of the Illinois village where Abraham Lincoln once resided, using this approach, and this is likewise the way in which I construct and perform much of my on-site ethnographic research.

In addition, as discussed in Chapter 7, tourists generate much of the sociocultural meaning that travel practices produce when off-site, post-visit, thus requiring a multisited approach that is a challenge to both design and accomplish. Since it is economically unfeasible to literally follow home every tourist one meets in order to gather information on post-visit meaning-making practices, other options must be employed. Although some of these options are not considered traditional to ethnographic methods, they can generate initial contacts with participants that can lead to sustained and rich engagement. Harrison (2003) placed newspaper ads in her local residence area, looking for research participants who had recently traveled internationally and traveled regularly. Respondents to the advertisements received a basic questionnaire regarding travel experiences that was used to select longer-term participants. She initially gathered data through videotaped open-ended interviews and time spent looking at and talking about photographs and souvenirs in their homes. Some of Harrison's participants sent her postcards and souvenirs from ongoing travels and copies of their travel journals, creating sustained relationships.

Although questionnaires are typically not a part of ethnographic research, mostly because of the dry, quantitative nature of most questionnaires, I incorporated one that included both quantitative and qualitative content regarding both on-site and post-visit practices and experiences. I gave this questionnaire to tourists whom I spent significant time with, usually over an hour, with the request that it was to be self-administered after they returned to their communities of residence and mailed back to me. I also exchanged email and postal addresses with hundreds of tourists (those that completed questionnaire plus a number of others) and continued contact and conversation with many of them for extended periods of time following our initial meetings in Manhattan. I still communicate with several via email and on-line social networking sites. My everyday and professional environments well beyond New York City also provided opportunities to meet and speak at length with even more people who had been to the WTC site, Oklahoma City, or similar commemorative historical sites. These tourists-returned-home could be found everywhere in my everyday life beyond the actual fieldsites that required travel away from my home community—at the gym, in the office, at academic conferences, among students in my classes, in airports, among family and friends. Such ongoing opportunities for research further extended my fieldsites temporally and spatially, creating numerous fieldsites that paralleled the ways in which tourists are dispersed post-visit while also blurring the often presumed boundaries between on-/off-site, work/personal life, and research/teaching.

THE TROUBLE WITH TOURISTS II: THE TOURIST AS "OTHER"

The lack of focus on tourists' actual experiences is also a result of other critical factors, ones that are as grounded as in the dominant academic paradigm constructed and uncritically reproduced by scholars of tourism as they are in issues of methodology. John Jakle (1985:3–4) notes that the earliest tourism scholars, including Relph (1976), Boorstin (1961), and Cohen (1974), perceived and represented tourists and tourism as characterized by inauthenticity, ignorance, gullibility, passivity, escapism, shallowness, having a lack of meaningful sociocultural value and function, and being culturally ignorant and destructive. These characteristics remain the primary ways in which tourists are most typically represented in the present, even when addressed within anthropology. For example, articles published in the 2005 special issue of the *National Association for the Practice of Anthropology Bulletin* on tourism, tourists, and anthropology duplicate this construction. Tourists are excluded as significant ethnographic participants in the articles, and when discussions of tourists are included abstractly and via broad generalizations, it is with the aim of using anthropology to rectify irresponsible tourist and tourism developers' behaviors and practices. I do strongly support such intervention in a great number of cases, particularly for ecologically or archeologically fragile destinations, in cases of massive power discrepancies between tourists and tourees (such as that in sex tourism), and in crafting and supporting community-based and sustainable tourism development. Yet this consistent reproduction of the notion that tourists and tourism are overwhelmingly negative—and that the anthropologist (or other academic researcher) is always superior to the tourist—is a result of the ways in which tourists have been either ignored or constructed as a new Other, albeit Others who are treated in ways that would be considered highly unacceptable if applied to our more "traditional" ethnographic subjects.

A major impetus for the study of tourism (but not necessarily tourists) in anthropology during the last quarter of the 20th century was the increasing inclusion of the traditional communities studied by anthropologists into the tourist landscape as the global tourism industry expanded into new locales at an increasingly rapid rate.[8] In the 1970s and 1980s anthropologists became increasingly concerned with how "their" communities "would fare against the arrival of tourists, unschooled in anthropology, who sought an authentic experience," and they saw "this 'invasion' as a part of the unwanted globalization process" (Wallace 2005:6–7). Although tourists were included in some ethnographic studies, the central topic of inquiry was largely limited to relationships between non-Western tourees (locals/"hosts") and Western tourists (non-locals/"guests"). The focus was not on the tourist experience but rather the experiences of and cultural impacts on locals. This approach is exemplified by one of the earliest volumes of work by anthropologists on tourism, *Hosts and Guests: The Anthropology of Tourism* (1989 [1977]), edited by Valene Smith. And despite the increasing presence of tourists and tourism in many fieldwork communities, as Crick (1995) and Bruner (2005) note, this particular impetus for culture change and form of culture contact was often obscured in other ethno-graphic publications of this time period. On this phenomenon, Bruner writes that

> tourists appear at our field sites as intrusive country cousins, or
> as Clifford Geertz (1996) put it, "messing up the neighborhood."
> They are found wandering around, taking photographs, and
> seeking travel stories, but most often they are left out of profes-
> sional monographs and articles. . . . The contemporary omission
> of tourists [as ethnographic subjects] is a similar phenomenon,
> a purposeful ignoring of that which is present but that ethnog-
> raphy finds embarrassing or threatening to its privileged pos-
> ition. (2005:8)

This phenomenon is best represented as a dichotomous con-struction of the scholar as knowledgeable Self and the tourist as the hopelessly ignorant Other, albeit the largely imagined and invented (rather than as actually lived) Other.

On the persistence of the Other as fundamental to both the ori-gins and ongoing work of anthropologists, Trouillot argues that the anthropologist is still "looking for the savage, but the savage has vanished"; thus "one could reinvent the savage, or create new savages in the West itself" (1991:35). Although not all tourism scholars are anthropologists or other types of social scientists, I assert that Trouillot's observation is an unnervingly accurate representation of the way in which scholars from many discip-lines, including anthropology, have canonized the "Western/ First World Tourist" writ large as a postmodern "new savage." This new "savage"/Other is primitive, ill-mannered, uncivilized, naïve, simultaneously passive, and terribly destructive, a "sav-age"/Other created in the West by the West and only begrudg-ingly (if that) acknowledged as a true part of the greater human society of the world, "West" or "Rest." The ways in which tourists as Others are represented is thus not so terribly different from those in some of the early accounts of indigenous and colonized peoples by missionaries, explorers, and government officials that informed the writings of armchair anthropologists. And as with the armchair anthropologists of the past, these representations are taken uncritically as true by those who do not engage directly with tourists in the process of collecting research data, further reproducing the academic construction of the tourist as savage Other. And while the primitive Other has historically been the favored ethnographic subject, the tourist as savage Other is of no interest—we think that we already understand this uncultivated member of the swarming, consumer masses. There appears no need to attend any further to their strange ways. We are instead enamored of the other face of the Tourist Other, the "traveler."

Trouillot offers the notion that the Other is fundamentally Janus-faced; one face is that of the savage or primitive and the other is that of "the West itself, but the West fancifully constructed as a utopian projection" (1991:28). In both scholarly studies of tourism and social distinctions held by some members of the broader traveling public, this particular utopian projection of the West is the well-meaning, bare-bones "traveler." The "traveler," taking the form of the socially responsible ecotourist, humanitarian aid vacationer, or backpacker who explores beyond commercialized paths and presumably treads lighter on both the landscape and foreign cultures, is an acceptable subject for research; he/she represents all that are "best practices" and "good" goals for travel in the eyes of intellectuals. The "traveler" is the new Noble Savage, worthy of study or at least commendation, whereas the bumbling, ignorant "tourist" is locked away on the destructive side of the savage slot, doomed to discourses of the unsalvageable tourist Other.

The "tourist" is constructed as Other through the terms used to describe, literally or metaphorically, what tourism and tourists fundamentally are and the social functions that travel is presumed to fulfill. MacCannell asserted that "tourist attractions are precisely analogous to the religious symbolism of *primitive peoples*" (1999 [1976]:2, emphasis added), with tourism being understood as a form of secular pilgrimage (Graeburn 1977). Decades later tourism as a social practice is still viewed similarly, understood by scholars as the modern equivalent to the "festivals and pilgrimages found in *more traditional*, God-fearing societies" (Graeburn 2004:25, emphasis added).[9] Typologies employed by some scholars, as well as nonscholars who travel for leisure, also represent this dichotomy. "Travelers" are considered distinct from tourists as an ideal type of peripatetic person, favored by scholars as civilized and implicitly representing the West in a utopian manner as the "right" and "ideal" way to travel in contrast to the ways that "tourists" travel. "Travelers" use local transportation, may stay with local residents, rarely (if ever) take photographs, might know some of the language, privilege authentic cultural experiences; they may also think they are "going native," as much as this is presumed to even be possible. "Travelers" are thought to wholly appreciate all aspects of authentic local culture, be it food, rituals, art, music, or the landscape.

In contrast, "tourists" take package tours, stay in lodgings that provide the familiar settings, comforts, and foods of home, take endless photographs and buy countless souvenirs, are ethnocentric— loathe to understand the local language and completely satisfied with whatever cultural performances they see, regardless of authenticity. If we were to compare the travels undertaken by anthropologists as a part of our work, we would insistently claim that we are far more like "travelers" than "tourists," even when we are marked as tourists by locals despite our insistence that we absolutely are not "tourists" even when we travel for leisure. Although anthropologists and other scholars would indeed likely self-identify as "travelers," the often denied similarities between anthropologists and tourists also inform the scholarly construction of tourists. MacCannell criticizes suppositions that social scientists are distinctly different from tourists, observing how

> tourists are criticized for having a superficial view of the things that interest them—and so are social scientists. Tourists are purveyors of modern values the world over—and so are social

scientists. And modern tourists share with social scientists their curiosity about primitive peoples, poor peoples and ethnic and other minorities. (1999 [1976]:5)

Malcolm Crick argues that the reason that tourists (and tourism) have been omitted in ethnographic works, included in works but disparaged, or been considered nonlegitimate topics for study is because the way in which "anthropological and touristic identities overlap . . . causes anxieties" (1995:208).[10] A most fundamental similarity is how both anthropologists and tourists "travel to collect and expropriate what they value from the other and then tell of their journeys" (Crick 1995:210), engendering various forms of cultural capital for both parties once returned to their respective communities of residence.

For tourists this cultural capital takes multiple forms: the spectacular stories they tell friends and family, the photographs they share, the souvenirs they display and give as gifts—all of which create status in the eyes of their intimate communities. For anthropologists this cultural capital is having material for scholarly publications and presentations required to properly advance one's academic career (Crick 1995:214). The production of this cultural capital is made possible for both anthropologists and tourists because of the same history of political economic processes, from colonialism and other forms of imperial conquest through the present, highly imbalanced international capitalist market system. Tourism and anthropology both "arise from the same social formation and are variant forms of expansionism occupying the space opened up by extensions of power" (Bruner 1989:439). Yet as Others/"savages," tourists are thus considered problematic, non-agentic, deluded, and ignorant, unworthy of much study beyond that which focuses on the problems that tourism brings about in the world. Working exclusively within this paradigm precludes the possibility of addressing any deep sociocultural significance that the practices of travel and tourism may engender for travelers themselves. As long as they remain understudied, we will indeed continue to have "very little theoretical certainty about tourism's effects on tourists themselves and the communities to which they return" (Wallace 2005:22).

As noted previously, some scholars have included tourists as a primary source, and some who have not do indicate the need for a more tourist-centered approach in future research. In his analysis of the ethnic and international simulacra employed at Busch Gardens and Disney's Epcot Center, Mintz calls for such an approach while also drawing specific attention to the problems with current paradigmatic, scholarly discursive construction of tourism, stating that

> we need to know far more about the tourist experience, its motives and functions, and its complex role in our society. One primary need is for more audience research, particularly qualitative, in which the participants themselves articulate their expectations and their sense of what they have experienced. However, it is a gross oversimplification to present the issues as one of the "real" versus "artificial" experience, or "learning" and/or "inspiration" versus recreation, amusement, or for that matter, of consumerism or leisure as a commodity. These distinctions are misleading and reductionist. (2004:185–86)

While he calls for a rejection of the some of the unproductive dichotomies that are at the heart of the problems with tourist-centered research, he does not take this call any further and offer possible alternatives. Mintz also notes that these dichotomies of "authentic versus artificial" and "learning versus amusement" are related to specific theoretical positions on consumption that underlie the ways in which many scholars fundamentally frame and interpret tourism as a social practice. Scholars' disinclination to take tourists seriously as agentic subjects is a result of binary frameworks that deny the possibility of consumption as having any positive, productive relationship to contemporary cultural identities, much less any meaningful historicities. Thus undertaking tourist-centered research requires a critical rethinking of how we regard consumption and commodities, two fundamental components to contemporary tourism and its array of social practices, in relation to human meaning-making.

The focus of this book is on how contemporary tourism, with its multiple forms of consumptive practices, plays a critical role in the social construction, production, and performance of commemorative heritage and historical sites and the making of collective and individual historicities and identities. If we are to begin to understand these constructive consequences of travel to commemorative sites for both travelers and for the sites, a critique of anticommodification perspectives and a cogent argument for understanding consumption as culturally constructive is thus required. Such a critique follows in the next two chapters, detailing the centrality of and limits to anticommodification perspectives for understanding travel to "dark" sites such as the WTC, cultural authenticity, and meaning-making. It is now time to begin unpacking the travel phenomena that have been designated as "dark tourism."

CHAPTER 3

Unpacking "Dark" Tourism

Whether it is touring concentration camps, tramping over First World War battlefields, or having your picture taken at Ground Zero, sadness sells holidays. Not any old sadness, mind. This is the good stuff, the kind that can be experienced secondhand. (Rowat 2002)

BODIES IN MOTION, BODIES AT REST

The former site of the WTC towers is a destination for tourist and local visitation both despite and because of the absence of the iconic twin skyscrapers that were once a key New York City tourist attraction. Whereas 1.8 million people visited the WTC complex in 2000, double that number—3.6 million—visited the space where the twin towers once stood during 2002 (ADNY 2003a:5). In 2003, 80% of domestic and foreign tourists to Lower Manhattan either visited the WTC site or included it in their planned itinerary (ADNY 2003b:21).[1] In a 2007 survey of hotel guests, the WTC was the top Lower Manhattan attraction among those visiting New York for the first time, with 75% visiting the site compared to 41.2% visiting the Statue of Liberty/Ellis Island and 39.7% visiting Battery Park/Castle Clinton (ADNY 2008:13).

Throughout the ongoing process of recovery and rebuilding in the aftermath of September 11, 2001, the WTC site has been a highly contested locus for both tourists and local visitors to witness history-in-process, memorialize the dead, and grapple with the reality of an unexpected, large-scale tragedy on U.S. soil. However, many locals, scholars, cultural critics, journalists, and everyday people consider tourists at the WTC site and in similar traumascapes of violence and disaster to be inappropriate and exploitative despite the prevalence of such places worldwide as commemorative heritage and historical sites. As mentioned in Chapter 1, popular and scholarly media treat visiting sites such as the WTC primarily as what John Lennon and Malcolm Foley call "dark tourism" (2000:1)—that is, a modern form of travel to "dark spots" (Rojek 1997:62), places of death, violence, and tragedy that are made amenable to tourism in some manner. According to this perspective, these sites have questionable social value, because they have, in some manner, been commodified for tourist consumption, and all forms of consumption are considered deficient in social value, meaningfulness, and authenticity. This position is also informed by a persistent ideology that "the very words tourist and tourism carry negative connotations" both inside and outside the academy (Jakle 1985:3). The negative connotations associated with tourists and tourism are derived, in part, from the basic fact that tourism is fundamentally a highly consumptive and commodified social practice.

In the popular media, tourists who visit the WTC site are often represented as engaging in behaviors inappropriate to a site of death and disaster, purchasing souvenirs or blithely treating their stop there as they would any of the other tourist sites in Lower Manhattan. One New York City travel website, despite listing the former WTC towers' site as a must-see destination, offered this scathing narrative:

> Tourism is alive and kicking in New York City. At least at Ground Zero. They plunk themselves in line and linger. The couple from Indiana standing in prayerful silence, the woman brushing away the occasional tear; the lardish man with the rumpled knock-off NYPD cap, pointing his fattish finger with excitement as he almost flies over the precipice of the platform. (Altebrando 2001)

Although some meaningful contemplation on the part of tourists is acknowledged, numerous media articles present a persistent discursive construction of non-locals at the site as "typical tourists," the savage Other. Tourists are described as being overweight, rude, and badly dressed; purchasing and flaunting cheap souvenirs; taking photographs while smiling; complaining about increased airport security; and treating the disaster site as though it were a place for entertainment.

Local journalists have also expressed the anger many New Yorkers had, and continue to have, over the site as a tourist destination as well as the commodification of 9/11. Dara Lehon wrote in Manhattan's *Downtown Express*:

> But for people visiting my city these days for its nightlife, culture, people, or even as a stop over to Atlantic City, Ground Zero seems to be just another stop on the N.Y.C. tour, squeezed in before heading to Canal St. for some bargains and Little Italy for gelato. And as with most things American, the "Ground Zero" and "September 11th" brands have been so successfully marketed even for natives, they'll sometimes roll off our tongues with as much feeling as the Yankees losing a game or Charlotte's converting to Judaism on *Sex and the City*. (2003)

This perspective positions tourists in sites of tragic events and places that memorialize such events as curiosity seekers, passively "gazing at someone else's tragedy" (Cole 1999:114), at just another stop on the tourist itinerary.

This particular understanding of tourism to "sites of the dead" is extremely ahistorical, if we consider that sights/sites of death constitute a significant number of travel attractions and destinations both past and present. Religious pilgrims, from the Middle Ages to the present, have traveled to shrines containing saints' remains, such as teeth, skulls, hand bones, death shrouds, and blood or other bodily fluids. The death, torture, burial, and imprisonment sites of saints are prominent destinations. The 18th-century Grand Tour included the ancient ruins of the Mediterranean and the Great Pyramids of Egypt; in the 19th century Thomas Cook included the Battle of Waterloo site in Belgium as a stop on one of his earliest package tours outside the United Kingdom. Before Disneyland's debut in 1955, the Forest Lawn Memorial-Park in Glendale (established in 1906 and the preeminent archetype for cemetery development and design in the 20th century in the U.S.) was southern California's top tourist attraction. Events of scale that result in death and destruction play a central role in the establishment of many existing and future sites for tourist visitation. International and civil wars in the past two and present centuries alone have produced a large number of the sites/sights, monuments, and museums that constitute tourist destinations worldwide. Valene Smith, a pioneer of tourism studies in anthropology, notes that "war stimulates promotional, emotional, military, and political tourism and that war-related tourism attractions are the largest single category [of tourist attractions] known," and it motivates memorabilia collection, reenactments, and visits to memorials (1998:202).

From war museums and battlefields to the final resting places of national leaders, the catacombs of Italy, art and history museums, Holocaust death camps, and heritage sites such as Colonial Williamsburg, the educational, cultural, and historical dimensions of tourism and tourist destinations are overwhelmingly centered on the dead. In acknowledging that such sites constitute much of the tourist terrain, Anthony Seaton writes: "it is hardly an exaggeration to suggest that in the midst of many tourism forms of life, we are in death" (1999:132). Yet can we unquestionably accept the assertions of Sandie Holguín (2005) and Lennon and Foley (2000) that World War battlefields became tourist sites primarily because people became inured to violence and death through the popular consumption of movie theater newsreels showing actual battles and bodies, engendering "dark" and morbid desires to see these sites first hand?

Heritage and historical sites that have their historical importance rooted in acts of violence and instances of death are also often and unfortunately treated by scholars (and in some cases, the public) as though their "true" and legitimate existence, cultural purposes, and social salience somehow lie beyond lived engagement with a broader public who are, more often than not, tourists.

When acknowledged at best, tourists are represented as passive spectators of these sites and, at worst, as destructive consumers whose motivations for visiting such sites are highly questionable, if not socially inappropriate. In contrast, I take tourism to play a central role in the literal and symbolic making and maintenance of historical places, in this case, those that are commemorative sites to violent events of scale. Tourists are understood here to be participating agents in the social production, consumption, performance, and construction of historically salient sites through various tourist and everyday practices, both during travel and post-travel. However, several issues that preclude the effectiveness of such an explanatory framework must be examined. This chapter begins addressing these issues through a critical analysis of the scholarly construction of "dark" tourism.

OF TRAUMASCAPES AND TRAVELERS: WHAT IS SO "DARK" ABOUT "DARK TOURISM"?

Scholars of tourism have recently begun to delineate tourist destinations that are sites of or places that represent death, violence, and disaster as part of a specific phenomenon: "thanatourism" (Seaton 1996; Sharpley and Stone 2009; Stone and Sharpley 2008), or more popularly and as previously noted, "dark tourism" (Lennon and Foley 2000).[2] Some of the sites discussed by these and other scholars (for example, Dann and Seaton 2001; Holguín 2005; Hughes 2008; Muzaini, Teo, and Yeoh 2007; Rojek 1993; Slade 2003; Smith 1996; Strange and Kempa 2003; Tunbridge and Ashworth 1996) include various war battlefields, genocide museums and prisons, Dealey Plaza, Kurt Cobain's suicide site, cemeteries, Gettysburg, Gallipoli, the death camps of Poland, Graceland, former slave-trade sites in Ghana, Jack the Ripper's haunts, the murder sites of Martin Luther King and John Lennon, Alcatraz, Waterloo, and the former homes of serial killers. To categorize such sites as "dark" tourism destinations is a problem for a number of reasons, not the least of which is how such an approach inadvertently collapses these sites onto a flat plane of value whereby Hiroshima is somehow isomorphic to a waxworks horror museum in terms of broad social and historical value simply because both are visited by tourists.[3] However, the primary problem is the academic construction of "dark tourism," the cultural conditions under which it is said to have emerged, and the motivations presumed to underlie this type of travel as truly distinct from authentic and meaningful historical, heritage, or cultural tourism.

All these sites may indeed be categorized as "dark" in the sense that they represent instances of violence and/or death, which by most Western perspectives are considered malevolent, negative, ghastly, and destructive. Yet tourism to such places is understood primarily in terms of the act of tourism itself being similarly "dark" and from "dark" motivations rather than anything positive and so-cially constructive. In scholarly discourse the term *dark tourism* first appeared in a 1996 special issue of the International Journal of Heritage Management edited by John Lennon and Malcolm Foley, professors of tourism studies at Glasgow Caledonian University.[4] Lennon and Foley (2000) and other tourism scholars broadly define "dark" tourism as travel to "fatal attractions" (Rojek 1993:136), "black spots," or "sensation sights" (Rojek 1997:62), sites/sights of death, disaster, or other tragic atrocities that have, in some manner, been commodified for tourist consumption.

Morbid tourism is another term used, encompassing both "sudden violent death . . . which quickly attracts large numbers of people" and "attraction-focused artificial morbidity-related tour-ism" such as museums of torture or waxworks (Blom 2000:32). Chris Rojek (1993, 1997) argues that the growing interest in these sites/sights derives from contemporary desires and demands for new kinds of escape through travel from the repetitious tedium of everyday life. Rojek also considers this to be a uniquely post-modern phenomenon that locates the media as the central means through which people actually "experience" and "witness" death in the present, be it in movies or the news, resulting in a vast cul-tural distancing from death that engenders an extreme and mor-bid curiosity about death and tragedy.

Drawing on the notion of thanatopsis, most broadly defined as the contemplation of or a meditation on death, dying, and the dead, Anthony Seaton characterizes "dark" tourism, or "thana-tourism," in his terminology to be "wholly or partially motiv-ated by the desire for actual or symbolic encounters with death" (1996:234). Seaton constructively argues in a subsequent work that what he classifies as thanatourism has a much deeper tem-poral history and this history is largely unacknowledged by other scholars of tourism at sites of death, disaster, and violence (1999:132). Five categories of sites and activities constitute Seaton's thanatourism typology:

1. witnessing public death-in-process (gladiator battles, pub-lic executions of past centuries, lynchings, fires, airplane crashes, sinking boats)
2. visiting sites of mass or individual deaths after they have occurred (Holocaust death camps, Pompeii, Graceland, Dealey Plaza)
3. visiting interment and memorial sites (cemeteries, cata-combs, war memorials)
4. seeing the material evidence or symbolic representations of deaths at locations other than their occurrence (museums and memorial monuments)
5. watching and/or participating in reenactments of death (the Passion Play at Oberammergau, battle reenactments) (1999:131)

While acknowledging that death may not be the only motivation for such travel, Seaton still maintains that travel to all these sites are forms of thanatourism, and they are fundamentally driven by desires for encounters with death, albeit with highly varying degrees of intensity or realistic representations of death.

However, thanatopsis, in its most basic form and true to its origins as a philosophical, religious, and literary concept, is not solely about individual desires for encounters with death and the dead, literally or symbolically. It is instead about the pro-cess of coming to accept death as a part of the life cycle through encounters with or reflection on death, the dead, often through the material and performative culture of death and dying. By this extended definition, visiting the Killing Fields of Cambodia or Dachau would serve the purpose of not only accepting death but, in the process of doing so, also relegating the dead to the inevitable progression of the human experience, rendering how and why they died irrelevant. War and genocide would thus be understood as deaths that are unavoidable, not to be feared, and certainly not something to be ameliorated or prevented in the future for any rational reason.

Such an understanding is precisely the opposite purpose that such historical sites are intended to serve as part of their preservation and use through visitation, particularly those that have been formalized as commemorative sites. Although not all visitors to Auschwitz-Birkenau, the Oklahoma City National Memorial, or the Kigali Memorial Center in Rwanda will come away from the visit fully internalizing and actualizing these sites' missions to "never forget" and "never allow this to happen again," to describe visiting such sites as a thanatopic is to deny that we can ever learn anything from the consequences of human violence. *Thanatourism* is therefore a fundamentally flawed term for describing tourism to sites of or that represent tragedy, and thanatopsis as the acceptance of death and dying is infrequently the result that visitation to such sites engenders.

Tourists at the WTC site articulate a wide range of motivations for visiting this site of tragedy, and they shared with me very diverse reactions to seeing what remains. Individuals' motivations to visit the site varied from "I had to see it to really know what happened, the news only showed the planes over and over and over" to "it's like when we went on the boat to the sunken ship at Pearl Harbor last summer . . . to pay respects and pray for the dead and their families." Some visitors have relative degrees of closeness to victims, people who had volunteered at the site, or rescue and recovery workers. Parents frequently expressed feeling an urgent need to come to the site to show their children a place they consider to be, in their words, "a terrible historic event," "part of American history . . . in our lives," and "something we hope our grandchildren will never have to see." The tourists in my research understand that, as Jakle notes, "in tourism, *seeing* for oneself is believing" (1985:2, emphasis added), and the act of physically bearing witness to the site as it exists at the moment of visitation makes more real the distant witnessing on and after 9/11 that transpired via the news media. In the cases of both the WTC and Oklahoma City sites, seeing these sites first hand provides tourists with a wider context for understanding the spatial and emotional magnitude of the tragedy in the present, something perceived by many non-local visitors as absent in their local media, both past and present.[5] The sense of curiosity that these visitors have is not one for seeing where people died and taking some kind of morbid pleasure in this act but a simple curiosity about what the site actually looks like to literally make the event real rather than as mediated through the news.

Seeing and experiencing the site also provides tourists the opportunity to reflect on what has transpired since 9/11 for individuals, the United States, and the world, particularly in terms of continued or impending death and dying. Jeffrey, an insurance company agent from Minnesota, shyly told me his story:

> I changed a lot since that day . . . lifestyle stuff, for my health, I had got really depressed, I couldn't stand thinking that this [September 11] was like the end of humanity. . . . I couldn't even keep up at work or sleep. So I went to a doctor for the first time in, um, fourteen years for help or something and he told me I was gonna have a stroke because of my blood pressure and I changed a lot of stuff . . . sort of here to give thanks for their sacrifice, yeah, I know that's sad, but I was born again. . . . I might have died if this hadn't of happened but I wish so many people didn't have to die.

He reflected on how his life and possible death were so closely linked to the events, not only making the WTC a national historical site and the events of 9/11 an important moment in his nation's history but also marking the event and the aftermath as having an even deeper emotional significance to him.

Some visitors ardently supported the military interventions in Afghanistan and Iraq, the search for Osama bin-Laden, the capture and execution of Saddam Hussein, and the war in Iraq and on terrorism writ large as "the right thing[s] to do" in response to 9/11. Yet others expressed new-found antiwar positions, uneasy ambivalence, or further reinforcement for continued resistance to "revenge retaliation" after seeing and experiencing the empty space once inhabited by thousands of living beings now dead. Diverse reflections on the various meanings accorded to human mortality (both their own and others'), rather than being a dark and morbid attraction to or an acceptance of death were recurring themes in these tourists' narratives. Local residents, like tourists, frequently iterated similar sentiments, even when they had visited the site many times. In contrast to locals who criticized tourism at the WTC, numerous others would bring out-of-town guests to see the site, acting as informal tour guides and narrating their recollections of the event, previous visits to the area, and how the site has changed over time.

As members of a very broad public, both locals and tourists at the site are interested stakeholders in the process of commemorating the dead and historicizing the event, and neither group expected the site to be pleasurable or entertaining. Nathan, a tourist from Florida, showed me the photos he took of the site on his camera phone, telling me how

> going down there wasn't like the other things we did, like going to the Letterman Show, I mean, shit, looking at that hole and flowers and names wasn't easy to do, but we had to do it, to see what it is like. . . . it's so real to me now, that this can really happen.

Tourists are engaging in the contemplation of death and dying and memorializing the dead, and through doing so, they are situating emotional and politicized selves in an ongoing narrative of local, national, and international tragedy and its aftermath, not enacting a disrespectful, "dark" attraction to the death of others. They neither were nor are presently in the process of becoming accustomed to or accepting of death; death, particularly violent and unexpected death, is greatly feared, and the dead are highly charged with social and historical meaning. If death were not so feared, the dead would have no measure of symbolic power; discourses of heroism, victimhood, sacrifice, and honor would be impossible to craft if the dead were as impotent as signs. As Peter Slade writes of Australian and New Zealander tourists at the battlefield of Gallipoli, the feelings they have "in respect to the dead . . . are not likely to be for the dead as about them" (2003:781). The dead are not simply individuals to be mourned but are constructed as representative of a significant moment in time that is processually rendered salient as a part of shifting national identities and historical patrimony. Additionally, advancing Slade's assertion about tourism at Gallipoli a step farther, I contend that visiting these sites of violence and death, in many ways, is even less about the dead and more about the living visitors/tourists and their own negotiated subject positions within and across various communities of identity and belonging, from the local to the international.

Nevertheless, scholars who analyze tourism to sites of death or disaster explicitly or implicitly assert that the motivations for visiting such sites center on a morbid and senseless curiosity, a culturally conditioned immunity to violence, desires for encounters with death, or a yearning for authenticity in a fragmented postmodern world. Further adding insult to injury, visitors to sights/sites of tragedy who are not surviving "victims or relatives of victims" are deemed "'casual' dark tourists" (Lennon and Foley 2000:169), discursively constructed as inconsequential in both intent and reaction, resulting in a hierarchy of meaningfulness and appropriateness based on a visitor's degrees of closeness to the tragedy.[6] Moreover, scholars presume that the various "dark" motivations for visiting such sites are unquestionably true and that they inhabit a continuum of equally valued motivations, some of which may be less negative (for example, Sharpley and Stone 2009).

This presumption is due, in part, to the previously discussed paradigm in tourism studies that focuses almost exclusively on every possible aspect of tourism and tourist destinations as primary subjects for study except for the actual tourists. This focus on the infrastructural, structural, and semiotic processes that produce tourist destinations such as historical sites, rather than tourists' experiences, has canonized certain fundamental definitions, categorizations, and presumptions about traveler motivations and experiences. It also calls into question the historical authenticity and salience of such sites, deeming any development of sites as amenable to visitation exclusively problematic as a means to uphold and reproduce the "negative anomaly" thesis that frames studies on "dark" tourism. Underlying this entire paradigm is a definition of authenticity that is problematically predicated on "the authentic" as free from the "profanity" of commercial activity and commodification.

THE SACRED AND THE PROFANE, THE "REAL" AND THE "DISNEY"

The existence of historical sites such as Pearl Harbor, the Oklahoma City National Memorial, and Gettysburg (to name only a few) are, as David Chidester and Edward Linenthal write, "intimately entangled in 'profane' enterprises as tourism, economic exchange, and development" (2001:1). However, scholarly works infrequently acknowledge tourists as participatory agents in place-making or tourism as often essential in the direct or indirect economic support of heritage sites, enabling their very existence in time, space, and memory. Public and scholarly discourses generally construct and codify tourism, as a form of economic exchange, to be undeniably "profane." In these discourses, tourists are most generally considered passive onlookers uncritically consuming prepared spectacles of history, and this consumption is considered particularly problematic when these are histories of violence—war, genocide, slavery, and other events of mass destruction, violence, and death, both past and recent. When constructive relationships among tourism, historical site production, and consumption are indeed acknowledged, the results of these relationships are often cast as a Disneyfication and commodification of tragedy, an erasure of authentic, "real history" in the most negative sense possible and a profaning of the presumed inherent sacrality of the dead.

The position that consumption is equivalent to an erasure of the "real" and to superficiality is foregrounded in Sharon Zukin's essay on New York City in the aftermath of 9/11. Writing on the WTC site, she says that "between the individual memories of horror and the *trivial act* of buying a souvenir, the city *disappears*" (Zukin 2002:20, emphases added). Similar articulations of an isomorphism between consumption and forgetting/sacrilege are also common in public discourses represented in the mass media. In addressing the sale of souvenirs at the WTC, a New York firefighter stated that "it is beyond insulting to this department, to this city, to this nation to allow that so close to such a sacred site. It's not going to become a mall. It's not a place to go shopping" (Hoffer 2002). In the opposition he made between a "sacred site" and "a mall," he is clearly articulating the perceived connection between entrepreneurial activity and sacrilege. Although retail outlets formed part of the original WTC towers complex and continue to exist in the adjacent World Financial Center buildings, debate has raged over whether or not shopping and food services will be included at the rebuilt WTC memorial and museum site, because the site has been sacralized by tragedy and through acts of public commemoration. While construction has been in process, the site proper has been denoted as an enterprise-free zone, and souvenir vendors line the sidewalks just beyond the east, north, and south street boundaries of whatever areas constitute the current commemorative loci for visitation. The general public, tourists, and journalists accept, begrudgingly tolerate, or actively malign the presence of commerce. Whatever is finally included at or immediately around the formal memorial will likely, for many, be considered unacceptable.

Acts of reconstructing other sites of tragedy and establishing memorial landscapes or museums are regarded by some as contributing to historical inauthenticity, trivialization, and a commercial exploitation of death and violence, because they include shopping and food facilities in addition to other tourist amenities. Tim Cole describes the reconstruction of Auschwitz I as a "Holocaust theme park"—an "Auschwitz-land" rather than a site of mass death (1999:100). He argues it to be so because of the presence of traveler's amenities: "tourist essentials . . . cafeteria, toilets, souvenir shop, cinema" as well as the architectural reconstruction of the site (Cole 1999:110–11). Likewise, John Beech notes that Buchenwald has both a restaurant and a bookshop, questioning when "these operations stop being seen as essential visitor support functions and begin to be perceived as tasteless and unacceptable exploitation of others' miseries" (2000:39).

Places of mass death are not the only sites criticized; sites where famous individuals died or are buried are also subject to this perspective. The inclusion of an art gallery, restaurant, and gift shop at Althorp, the childhood home and now burial site of Princess Diana, leads Thomas Blom to speculate that the site will develop into a "Dianaland" or "Dianaworld," and he considers the visitors who come to pay respects as participating in "morbid tourism" (2000:35). In the shop at the Sixth Floor Museum at Dealey Plaza, the presence of a child's paper doll book containing images of John F. Kennedy, Jackie Kennedy, and their children that "allows the reader to dress and undress" the Kennedy family as well as souvenir items such as key rings and T-shirts is evidence to Lennon and Foley that the Museum's "educative mission is clearly compromised" (2000:95). Not only does the presence of various tourist amenities and souvenir commodities "Disney-fy" a site and event, but violations of the "authentic" also take place through acts of site restoration and event representation. This exemplifies an uncritical acceptance of the idea that

> the greater the intervention at historic places, the greater the manipulation. And the greater the manipulation, the greater the contrivance. As we stray from strict preservation, we come nearer to pure entertainment and ultimately the land of the imaginary. (Sellars 1990:18)

Such a perspective posits that "the authentic" cannot survive commodification and that consumption of any kind is thus socially meaningless, if not downright destructive.

According to this perspective, any sort of entrepreneurial activity at, museological intervention in, or reconstructions of sites and violent events results in diminished social value and meaning, trivialization, and forgetting. Tourist visitation to and consumption of sites/sights of death and violence are thus cast as a negative practice that Disney-fies violent events rather than working in the service of creating and reproducing individual and collective social memories and historicities through physical, experiential encounters with these sites/sights. Why is Disney a recurring theme when memorial landscapes (both those in-process and those that have been formalized) and commemorative museums are discussed? Although it has become somewhat clichéd to invoke Disneyland as the antithesis to everything authentic and meaningful, the name of this fantasy park persists as shorthand for what Landsberg identifies as scholars' and "middle-brow journalists'" perception of a "threat posed by an experiential mode of knowledge to the hegemony of the cognitive" (1997:76).

Concerned with how the United States Holocaust Memorial Museum has repeatedly been subjected to scholarly criticisms regarding the experiential nature of many of its exhibit spaces as "entertainment" rather than "proper history," Landsberg argues that

> it is reductive to presume that a museum or a movie, simply by trying to engage spectators physically as well as cognitively, irresponsibly conflates history and entertainment. In fact, the popularity of this new genre of experiential museums reflects a change in what counts as knowledge . . . [it] reflects the ways in which "new technologies of memory" alter the mechanisms by which individuals come to acquire knowledge. If experience, as I describe it, becomes increasingly important in the popular acquisition of knowledge, then a blurring between the boundaries of "entertainment" and "history" might not be a purely negative event. (1997:76–77)

Building on Landsberg's argument, I posit that the enduring invocation of Disneyland is also a product of how positions that devalue experientiality as frivolous "entertainment" do so not only by privileging cognitive knowledge[7] but also by associating such experientiality exclusively with all manner of commodities and practices of consumption. An association between experientiality and the consumption of commodities implies that the experiences simply can not be deeply meaningful, authentic, or socially productive; in the case of the WTC, such an association engenders fears that the site is not now and will fail to become a properly sanctified historical and commemorative site. The site is seen as a commodity in and of itself, because non-local people visit the site, souvenir vendors and other forms of commerce exist in the area, and corporate and civil organizations have created a shifting landscape of memorial installations intended for public consumption as the site moves toward formalization.

"NINEELEVENLAND"

Despite the establishment of shifting formal temporary and permanent commemorative elements, the millions of tourists who move through the WTC site engender in some people an opinion that tourists treat the place as though it were a theme park rather than a memorial site. Media discourses represent this opinion through clever but disparaging satires of the site as theme park, representing deep anxieties and fear that the WTC site is not now and will fail to become a properly sanctified commemorative site. Some critics create virtual 9/11 theme parks online, manufacturing marketing slogans, outlandish rides, and souvenirs such as:

> The GT Coaster! Wow! What a coaster! Snake your way around the rubble and get the best look at WTC site yet! Better put that camera away quick, though. We're headed for a 100+ story drop!!! And . . . we've got everything from Beanie Babies to pogs. . . . And we didn't forget about the adults. Try to hide your snicker when your mate puts on our WTC site® edible undies, with our logo, well, you know where![8]

Other non-existent theme park fantasy rides and souvenirs also appear in Ted Rall's editorial cartoon (Figure 3.1), side-by-side with Libeskind's Freedom Tower and the exposed slurry wall, both significant material and symbolic landscape elements in the rebuilding plans. Along with the already iconic Freedom Tower,

Rall's editorial cartoon presents the "Freedom Falls" ride, modeled after the water luge and "wild river" rides commonly found in North American amusement parks. It parodies real, existing souvenirs and other commemorative commodities sold throughout the tourist sites in Manhattan. Instead of a "United We Stand" logo baseball cap, a popular item found not only at the WTC site but across the United States, Rall's tourist wears one that says "United We Bland," critiquing the mass-produced, patriotic "United We Stand" paraphernalia that saturated the United States shortly after September 11.

Rall also criticizes the selling of souvenirs and commemorative items in general, presenting "victim dust" as a highly inappropriate and clearly morbid commodity available for purchase, a metaphor for all souvenirs sold on or near these grounds where people died. With a cynical nod to the American supershopper and the mall-riddled U.S. landscape, Rall also includes a "Mall of the Martyr." While an effective critique of unbridled commerce, this elides the past and present existence of extensive retail commerce at or near the site. The underground levels of the WTC once housed an extensive shopping mall of over 400,000 square feet, the largest mall on the entire island of Manhattan. The mall housed mainstream, national retail outlets including Ann Taylor, a Warner Bros. store, J. Crew, the Gap, Lenscrafters, and Victoria's Secret. Directly across from the WTC site on Church Street, the famous Century 21 department store remains today, having seen an incredible rebound in business since reopening on February 28, 2002, rather quickly after the events of 2001. Yet because this entire area is now a place of death, commercial activities are a topic for persistent debate and criticism.

The name that Rall chose for this imagined mall, "NineElevenLand," clearly signifies the perceived disjuncture between commerce and commemoration and the ongoing battles over controlling or completely excluding commerce at the present and future site because it is now a graveyard. The debates over commerce at the site began with the rebuilding plans that privilege new corporate office space as the most pressing aspect of the site's rebuilding and that now extend to retail services. Even if

Figure 3.1 Editorial cartoon by Ted Rall, *The New York Times*, January 12, 2004 (© Ted Rall. Used by permission of Universal Uclick. All rights reserved.)

the establishment of a cultural and performing arts center and memorial museum is realized, the controversy remains about whether the inclusion of cafés or gift shops in these locations is appropriate for the site and whether (or even how) to include the retail services once in the twin towers among the new buildings.

The cartoon's "Burger America" sign is likewise interesting, not only as a representation of food services as inappropriate commerce but also, ironically, because there is indeed a Burger King restaurant at the southeast corner of the WTC site, directly across Liberty Street. Until the iconic "Cross" was removed in 2006 and later relocated down the street outside St. Peter's Church, the restaurant's second floor provided a view of "The Cross" that was unobstructed by the viewing-wall fence.[9] During this time the space in front of the second-floor window was continuously full of visitors taking photographs, becoming a part of the memorial site itself in a rather unusual, and according to restaurant employees, a very unexpected way. Like "Burger America," the name that Rall bestows on this imagined theme park, "NineElevenLand," is unabashedly drawn from existing businesses and, in this case, the Disneyfication discourses of scholars and intellectuals and the public acknowledgment of Disneyland as one of "The" tourist meccas of and premier landscapes of contrived artificiality in the United States. The general tone of the cartoon aptly critiques both unrestrained consumerism and out-of-control patriotic jingoism; however, this tone is achieved through a degradation of non-local visitors: tourists caricatured in an imagined WTC theme-park environment, festively enjoying themselves at the expense of the event's victims.

Although the current rebuilding efforts have indeed made the WTC site amenable to tourist visitation, tourists are still perceived as defiling the site not only with their current presence but also with the "threat" of their future presence in the formalized commemorative site, particularly when engaging in consumption. Narratives from blogs and internet fora that discuss tourists at the site are cast in a negative tone, further situating tourists as "visiting a theme park," replete with photo opportunities and a selection of souvenirs. One online posting by a local Manhattanite on a WTC site forum described this "typical" scene, which may or may not have actually been witnessed:

> Like a scene from an amusement park, tourists parade about with their fanny packs and digital cameras, some stopping for family photos, others huddled around the countless "souvenir" stands fiddling with the latest 'in-the-moment" patriotic trinkets: WTC site hats and shirts, figurines and statues, key chains, pens, buttons, glass snow shakers . . . hot dog stands have doubled, and ice cream stands frequent Church St. on hot afternoons, giving families a chance to enjoy a delicious Choco-Taco while peering inside a pit where 2,800 people burned to death.[10]

Rides, souvenirs, food, and the common act of taking photographs are elements of "theme parks" in the paradigmatic sense and, when taken together or separately, construct a perception that tourists at the WTC site are taking part in frivolous and trivializing activities. Such a perception does not understand that tourists are engaging with the site in deeply meaningful, more serious ways. It completely disallows such an understanding. Yet these practices of consumption can indeed be found at almost all kinds of tourist sites, be they historical, commemorative, cultural, or designed for pure pleasure, such as resorts.

According to Mark Gottdiener, the touristic consumption of space and place takes place through shopping, both for "trinket" souvenirs and more everyday items while in the non-everyday spaces of tourism, but it is also "clearest in the stereotypical tourist activity of picture taking" (2000:269). In the media and in popular local opinion, picture taking by tourists is one of the most harshly disparaged visitor activities at the WTC site.[11] Some people find the act of photography to be inappropriate to a site of death even though there are no dead bodies there or other notable physical evidence of tragedy. In an article in *The New York Times*, Lower Manhattan resident Patricia Moore criticized tourists snapping photos, saying: "This is not Disneyland . . . [t]his is not Mickey and his friends. Why do they need to take a picture of that!" (Archibold 2003), invoking the incongruence between the pleasure spectacle of Disneyland and the somber grounds of the

WTC and calling into question the fundamental motivations for taking photographs at a place where mass destruction and death took place.

Others simply find tourist photography at the site to be a fundamentally unproductive social action. A section of graffiti, found in 2003 on the construction panels lining the Liberty Street walkway along the south border of the site, admonishes photo-taking tourists, stating: "We are all victims of hate. We are all survivors of what is America. Stop smiling into the camera and do something" (Figure 3.2). This statement articulates a sentiment that time spent at the site taking photographs should be used to "do something" as though personally witnessing, experiencing, and documenting the aftermath is "doing nothing." As discussed in later chapters, the act of photography and the photographs themselves are quite powerful, particularly as visual material culture for both making and evoking memories.

From the basic act of physical site visitation to taking photographs and buying souvenirs, touristic activities thus constitute a set of social practices that are considered by many to be negative, trivial, and profane. Yet although tourists come and go by choice,

Figure 3.2 Graffiti in the Liberty Street walkway
(© Joy Sather-Wagstaff 2003)

the vendors who sell them souvenirs day in and day out have been particularly singled out as targets for the wrath of both scholars and the public. In these discourses the necessity for such commerce around the site is questioned, vendors are often vilified as opportunists cashing in on tragedy, and the souvenirs are viewed as meaningless but, paradoxically, powerfully sacrilegious commodities. Underlying these discourses, theories of "dark tourism," and fears of Disneyfication is an intellectual and scholarly conception of consumption as passive, meaningless, and fundamentally inauthentic, avoiding the question: Can consumption be otherwise understood? To begin considering tourism as playing any role in the social construction of commemorative sites, it must be understood differently.

CHAPTER 4

Consumption, Meaning, Commemoration

Booklets, pins, flags, postcards, and gold-plated crosses like the one propped up on the World Trade Center site are just an offering of what can be bought at WTC site. Cross opportunists think of this flowering of blood-stained capitalism as a means of "healing" and "regenerating" the area. It is simply disrespectful and heartless, and by no means do residents feel comfortable passing the Disneyland-size crowds. . . . I'm sure none of the proceeds of any of these enterprises are going to charities or funds associated with the 11th. (http://groundzerothemepark.com)[1]

At WTC site itself, we joined hundreds of other onlookers winding our way around the massive city block which is now a hole. Being there gave us a totally different perspective from what we see on television . . . helping New York to recover [by visiting and spending money] is a wonderful way to help us recover as well. (Bischoff 2002)

Do Your Part—Fight Back NY! Spend money! (Fashion Center Business Improvement District banner, 2001)

COMMEMORABILIA: COMMODITIES FOR COMMEMORATION

As indicated in the first epigraph, street vending around the WTC site is seen by some as a form of insensitive opportunism and "blood-stained capitalism." In contrast to the perspective of the visitor in the second epigraph, those who purchase these items are perceived as demonstrating disrespect for both the dead and survivors, because they are not only encouraging this opportunism but also engaging in vulgar consumerism instead of "proper" acts of commemoration. The third epigraph generates a curious paradox in juxtaposition to the others. This is the text from a 2001 streetlight banner in Manhattan's Fashion District created by the Fashion Center Business Improvement District (FCBID). The FCBID launched the "Fight Back" campaign in October 2001 urging New Yorkers to avenge the destruction of the WTC by shopping and dining out locally at businesses suffering from the sharp post-9/11 decline in tourism to the city. In discussing this paradox of commemorative consumption, Molly Hurley and James Trimarco aptly state that the vendors are at the WTC site because "visitors [tourists] represent a large and willing market for all sorts of items . . . [it is a] commercial opportunity as well as a historical site" (2004:52).

In analyzing the "high moral drama" resulting from the simultaneous commemorative and commercial activities taking place at the WTC site, Hurley and Trimarco note that this "drama" is frequently (and mistakenly) characterized by two extreme representations. For some, vendors are "symbols of the spirit of trade and entrepreneurship that is connected to tropes of American patriotism," whereas for others, including the police who enforce conduct at the site as well as some tourists and locals, they are "representations of crass capitalism" (2004:53).[2] A closer look at what is actually happening at the site with these vendors reveals a far more complex reality than that represented by these dichotomous perspectives, dispelling some of the assumptions made by those who either have not been to the site or are not aware of the bureaucratic aspects of street vendor work and the culture of street commerce in Manhattan.

First, during the years when I was on-site, no licensed tables of souvenirs or food vendors were present on the WTC site proper; that is, the sidewalks that abutted the viewing wall around the site. One could walk the entire WTC site proper—from the WTC transit station and all the way through the World Financial Center on the west side—without encountering any souvenir salespeople other than those few that were on foot and selling goods illegally. Since the viewing wall was opened to the public in 2002, selling items on the sidewalks along the wall has been actively restricted (see Figure 4.1). One may see a few individuals in this enterprise-free zone carrying small book bags with one item for sale, usually a flip book of reproduced photographs or the ubiquitous "Day of Terror" booklet, both of which visually narrate the events of 9/11 chronologically at the Pentagon, Manhattan, and Shanksville, Pennsylvania, event sites. They walk through the crowds in a very surreptitious manner, because they are subject to warnings from or forcible removal by the New York Police Department (NYPD).

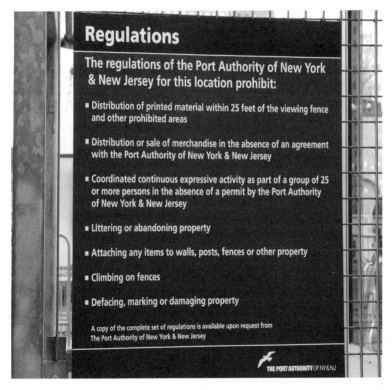

Figure 4.1   Port Authority of New York and New Jersey sign on the WTC viewing wall (© Joy Sather-Wagstaff 2007)

Souvenir vendor tables, hot dog carts, and ice cream trucks were generally located across and beyond the streets that line the WTC site: to the north of Church and Vesey, to the south of Church and Liberty, on Broadway across from St. Paul's Chapel, and along the rear fence of St. Paul's along Church, across from the viewing wall and the transit station. Before the renovation of Liberty Plaza Park (and name change to Zuccotti Park), souvenir tables (Figure 4.2) also populated the eastern and northern edges of the plaza area, interspersed with food and sundries vendors that catered primarily to local downtown workers. Farther away from the site, the sidewalks continued to be filled with vendors, mostly those selling items to locals (such as purses, sunglasses, fiction books, toys, candy, fruit, costume jewelry, incense, perfume, DVDs, and cell phone, PDA, and iPod accessories) with a few souvenir tables interspersed.

Second, street commerce in New York City was and remains highly regulated by the city and actively monitored by the NYPD.

Figure 4.2   Vendor tables at Liberty Plaza (Zuccotti) Park, adjacent to the WTC site (© Joy Sather-Wagstaff 2003)

Vendors are required to have licenses, although unlicensed vendors, on foot and carrying goods such as knock-off designer purses and pirated DVDs in sheets or sunglasses, watches, and cell phone accessories in briefcases, abound throughout Manhattan. In addition, beginning with the 2003 9/11 anniversary commemorative ceremony, vendors were restricted from setting up in their usual places across the streets from the site and were instead located a few blocks north, south, or east of the site if they worked that day.

Third, as part of a crackdown on vendors who claimed that their goods were being sold to benefit charities to increase sales, the city required anyone who was indeed selling such items be registered as a legitimate organization with the New York State Charity Bureau. While selling, these particular vendors were required to prominently post information about the specific charity along with their registration number. During my fieldwork period in 2004 I saw only one such licensed vendor who was selling "Save the Cross" T-shirts to support one of the organizations whose goal is to secure the inclusion of the "Cross" in the future formal memorial landscape

The licensed vendors[3] around the WTC site with whom I became familiar had perspectives on both their jobs and the visitors who bought the souvenirs they offered that were very diverse and different from those of journalists and cultural critics. With people gathered around their tables, they would tell me their stories, compliment and critique the tourists while breaking narrative stride every so often to find a T-shirt in the correct size, call out a price, collect money, or give a brief WTC history lesson to a tourist. After spending time with several regular vendors and hearing the stories of how they came to be vendors, I noted that the ways in which vendors were represented in the media, by some locals, and by cultural critics did not match their lived experiences in their occupation. I learned that many were living in homeless shelters, residing in halfway houses, or sharing tiny apartments with several other vendors, and most were not self-employed but working for large vending companies (see also Hurley and Trimarco 2004). These men and women neither were crass opportunists nor were making enormous profits; they were earning meager to reasonable daily or weekly pay often based on a very small percentage of sales totals. In contrast, their managers, who drive new model vans that carry the goods and vendors to their sites, often do quite well. The vendors who were self-employed tended to have longer histories of working in street commerce in this part of Lower Manhattan than did those who worked for vending managers, made a decent but not exorbitant living, and carried with them a proud sense of ownership about the area.

Although some vendors were very assertive, actively pitching their merchandise, others felt that this kind of salesperson showmanship is not appropriate for places close to the WTC site. In 2002 Jamal, a soft-spoken young man in his early 20s, sat patiently a few days a week at a table of books, postcards, photographs, and key chains often set up on the shady sidewalk outside St. Paul's Chapel, across from the WTC site. On the first day we met, we talked for about two hours, and every time someone paused at the table, he excused himself from our conversation and greeted the person. After apologizing for the interruptions several times, he explained that he worked for a company running souvenir tables from Battery Park to Times Square, and his manager checked in on him at least once a day to see how sales were going. If he did not meet daily sales goals set by his manager, Jamal took home a smaller percentage of the sales money, and managers pressured vendors to actively pitch the souvenirs to all passersby, regardless of where they were vending. Nevertheless, he did not try to "hook" potential buyers but waited for them to approach the table and touch the merchandise before speaking.

Jamal explained his adversity to being pushy like some other vendors and why he was "pretty okay" with making less money on the few days when he worked close to the WTC site:

> I just don't like hollerin' at people like some of these guys waving this stuff [tapping the booklets] in the air . . . they got no respect. I don't mind talking to folks when they come up [to the table], most of them are really nice and I get to meet people

CHAPTER 4

from all over but I ain't gonna be acting like some damn door hawker for a nudie club. That's not right for this place. When I work sometimes down on Broadway or in the park [Battery Park] I'll really try and sell you a whole lot of something! But not here. Be quiet and nice, respect all that [pointing towards the empty space behind the fence] sell some bad history to some nice people. They got to know and remember too.

When working at this location, he felt uncomfortable promoting souvenirs to those just passing by, believing that he was doing a better kind of service by more tactfully providing "bad history to nice people" who bought his goods. Jamal also knew that on the days he was not assigned this spot, someone else less respectful might be, and his concerns about a little less money were eased by knowing that, unlike some of his fellow vendors, he was acting respectfully. Once someone showed interest, he did pitch his items quite strongly, standing up and opening the books or collections of photographs, narrating the various images to the potential buyer and noting prices. Jamal did not want to risk losing this job, and he was acutely aware that his thin work experience and young age did not make him an ideal candidate for many work opportunities, particularly while the city remained in very slow process of economic recovery.

The recession that plagued New York after 9/11 hit the perpetually underemployed and under-skilled workers such as Jamal very hard, and it drastically affected other vendors who had been working at and around the WTC for many years selling both tourist souvenirs and the assorted sundries that locals purchase before and after work and during breaks. Self-employed vendors who wished to continue work in street commerce close to the WTC site were forced to change their products and strategies in order to survive in a suddenly altered and now ever-changing landscape as well as deal with continuing to work in a business that was now considered disrespectful by many. This happened to Sam and Benny, two middle-aged men, who ran a series of their own souvenir tables around the WTC site that shifted in position as pedestrian sidewalk access changed in the area. Hats, T-shirts, and key chains were their mainstay items, with a few crystal paperweights, sunglasses, sets of photos, and disposable cameras set out with the other merchandise.

One summer afternoon during a lull in business after the lunchtime rush, Sam and Benny told me the story of how they came to sell souvenirs at the WTC site and how they felt about this line of work:

SAM: I've been working here or somewhere nears here [the WTC area] for oh, like seven, eight years [the 1990s]. Been around all here for a long time. Lots longer than most. Licensed, too, the whole time.

JOY: What did you do before that?

SAM: I worked for the post office, good money, good hours but, man, I got tired of walking around all day! My brother sold stuff down here and I got to working with him and just retired from the post office. My pop, he worked steel on the towers so I kinda feel like I belong here anyhow. And I don't mind the standing or the talking, just the walking.

JOY: Did you sell New York T-shirts and souvenirs back then?

SAM: Oh, nah, mostly stuff people, workers around here all the time needed. Kids' books, batteries, pens, sunglasses, those crossword books, doo-dads, sometimes flowers on Fridays for dates, you know [*winking and smiling*]. Some New York stuff like that [*indicating the classic white "I♥NY" T-shirts*], maybe some [disposable] cameras but mostly for the workers.

BENNY: And me, I got this job because my cousin had a table and he got sick, sold cell phone stuff. I needed a job so I sold for him. We couldn't come down here for a long time in 2001, after. That's when I met Sammy.

SAM: Yeah. Yeah. Sold up in midtown for awhile, had to combine forces 'cause everyone [other vendors] was up there 'cause no one was here. Most people who work outside don't like working indoors, can't do it so there's not much else to do. Me, I gotta be outside. Gotta eat too you know!

JOY: That's why you came back here—too much competition up there?

BENNY: [*waving his hands around*] Sammy had a serious stake here, working down here so long, figured time to take it back . . . yeah, too many damn people everywhere else selling everything too! A lotta the legit [licensed] people didn't want to come here anyways. People were real mean to them.

SAM: Couldn't sell the old stuff so we sorta started over. Only the New York, fire department, [Trade Center] tower stuff now. It's all right stuff, good stuff, nothing disrespecting. People want it so we sell it. I guess they need this stuff, too. I get sad though. This isn't the same place anymore. There's a lot of faces I miss all the time, all the time, real nice people.

Unlike Jamal but similar to some of the other vendors I met, these two had been engaged in street vending before 9/11, and kin connections often formed the means of entry into the vending business. Like others who had worked in the area before, they validated their presence by their longer history of vending around the WTC, articulating a certain territoriality and ownership of the space past and present that meant a great deal to them far beyond the economics of making a decent living.

Sam had even more personal and intimate attachments to the site in the form of emotionally difficult associations felt most poignantly when he was remembering and missing a certain frequent customer or regular passerby who had always offered up a friendly hello. This and other stresses of working in this space post-9/11 had both of them regularly mentioning early retirement or getting more help to run their tables so that they could reduce their working hours. Sam and Benny both remarked on separate occasions that sometimes people are still mean to them, telling them to "get a real job" instead of profiting from the dead, but, for the most part, the locals and tourists who buy items will thank them for being there. Like Jamal, Sam and Benny perceived themselves as providing a service by selling products that both sellers and buyers see as representing an important moment in history, products I call "commemorabilia."

In discussing 9/11-related items for sale on eBay, Mick Broderick and Mark Gibson similarly acknowledge that the commerce in such 9/11 and WTC mementos and souvenirs "may have enabled thousands, perhaps hundreds of thousands, literally to bring the event home, to weave it into the fabric of their everyday lives" (2005:206). In contrast to those who view the sale of souvenirs solely as denigrating the events, victims, and aftermath of 9/11, this is a significantly different perspective on the social effects of consumption and commodification. This particular perspective is also one that I find far more productive for understanding how some commodities do indeed matter in various constructive ways. However, the issue of the uneasy relationships among tourism, consumption, commodification, authenticity, and memory in relation to historical sites in general remain to be untangled.

CONSUMPTION, AUTHENTICITY, AND PLACES FOR MEMORY

Mark Gottdiener views consumption as "the central focal interest of people in advanced industrial societies and the cornerstone today for the construction of identity" (2000:ix).[4] Yet the ways in which consumption and commodification are understood and framed all too often conclude that the identities constructed through consumption are illusory, inauthentic, superficial, and thoroughly "McDonaldized" or, at minimum, grossly homogenized. Given that tourism as a social practice is thoroughly grounded in acts of consumption and commodification, tourist activities are also considered suspect in terms of having "true" meaningfulness and social value, and scholarly theories of inauthenticity are asserted with even more force when tourism involves engagement with particularly powerful national and/or religious histories.

In criticizing the "authenticity" of contemporary Jewish and Protestant religious tourism in Israel, Noam Shoval asks

> if a tourist flies in a commercial jetliner, rides around in a Volvo bus or rented car from one of the big auto makers, sleeps at

a franchised Holiday Inn or Howard Johnson hotel, eats at a McDonald's or a Mövenpick restaurant, and visits audio-visual displays and themed, artificially simulated environments, what is left of the "authentic" aspect of the religiously inspired journey? (2000:262)

This question is posed to readers as though it is somehow realistically possible for the contemporary tourist to travel to and stay in Israel by exclusively using the "authentic" means of the past. Shoval then concludes by claiming that "the contemporary development of [simulated] sites relevant to religious tourism in Israel may seriously *undercut the significance* of the authentic historical locations and *trivialize* their meaning" (2000:262, emphases added). Unfortunately, Shoval provides a very thin description of two of the simulated sites that he sees as trivializing, "Time Elevator—Jerusalem" (a destination where film, motion platform seating, and special effects are used to present 3,000 years of Jerusalem's history up to the 1967 Six-Day War) and "Nazareth Village (a recreation of Nazareth in the 1st century).[5] In addition, he does not begin to fully articulate the complex significance of other, perhaps "more authentic" historical sites to various communities of belonging.

The perception that travel for pilgrimage, in its most traditional religious and ritualistic sense, has always been and should continue to be outside of the realm of consumption and commodification is an extremely persistent one in tourism studies. With a discomfort not unlike that which Shoval expresses over the presence of McDonald's and Holiday Inn hotels in Israel, other scholars likewise demarcate consumptive behavior and the presence of commodities as profane and thus absolutely oppositional to the sacred nature of religious pilgrimage. Sharon Gmelch, in her introductory essay to a reader on tourism and tourists, described her first encounter with religious pilgrimage at the Shrine of Knock in Ireland, a site where apparitions of the Virgin Mary, Joseph, and St. John the Evangelist appeared to local residents in 1879:

I was unprepared for the casual jollity of the pilgrims on the train from Dublin and taken aback by the commercial bustle of Knock's main street as people who had finished their prayers jostled with vendors to buy all manner of sacred and secular souvenirs—from plastic Marys meant to be filled with holy water to tacky T-shirts. (2004:6)

Although Gmelch does not discuss this any further, she is clearly taken aback because of a standing perception that cheerful behavior and buying souvenirs are sacrilegious when performed in spaces dedicated to sacrality. She was prepared to see only solemn pilgrims who presumably did not engage in commodity consumption and secular, if not downright jolly and thus profane, behaviors while on pilgrimage. Yet consumption is a fundamental characteristic of religious pilgrimage past and present; the differences lie in the scale of such consumption and the production of commodities related to pilgrimage. In the past it was primarily the wealthy who had the means to travel, and the impact that pilgrimage had on long-distance trade and the prosperity of numerous communities is akin to that which contemporary mass tourism has brought to the world and local economic markets in the 20th century. Hospices and inns providing lodging for pilgrims multiplied and flourished (bringing in monies to both religious orders and individual entrepreneurs), and a brisk market in religious souvenirs and counterfeit relics developed. Pilgrim badges, typically metal buttons purchased and worn post-pilgrimage on the brim of a hat or pinned to a cloak as a means to nonverbally communicate to others that one has completed a pilgrimage, are not so drastically different from today's souvenir T-shirts.

Competing claims on the burial sites and remains of saints and other holy persons often escalated to violence and calculated intrigue, because the faction who was lucky enough to end up with those remains or the oversight of a burial site would benefit economically as well as spiritually. Certain pilgrimage routes became central to broader identities beyond just religious ones; one good example is that of Santiago de Compostela, which endures into the present as a religious, historical, and national geography for multiple communities of belonging. Given this history, past and present historical and heritage sites for both national and religious histories, including commemorative sites, should be recognized as unconditionally embedded in travel and its related consumptive practices rather than disconnected from them. Consumption and commodification are indeed fundamental attributes of pilgrimage both past and present.

Perspectives viewing consumption and commodification as superficial and potentially degenerative to the "authentic" also extend to discussions on the embodied ways that sites are experienced by tourists. The "tourist gaze" (Urry 1990:1) and its related visual technology, tourist photography, are often central in these discussions; both the "gaze" and photography are understood to be about control through possession, a one-way relationship between powerful tourists and disempowered objects and "othered" people as objectified, consumable culture. Urry's tourist gaze is a systematic, socially organized way of seeing. The tourist gaze is passive in that it is a process of consuming sights/sites without much questioning of the construction of such sights/sites. The tourist gaze is also a form of domination in that it is enacted by tourists, a privileged class of people, visually consuming less privileged Others. The gaze is also assumed to be preformed, as are the objects of the gaze—primarily through various media—and the objectification of that which is gazed on is a form of imperialism for the purpose of consumption. For Urry the visual is the privileged means for consuming sites/sights, and the gaze is made material and circulated socially through acts of tourist photography.

The social production and construction of both tourist and everyday spaces and places are dependent on the consumption of such spaces and places. However, the tourist consumption of places is often discussed only in terms of destruction, both literal and symbolic. One such perspective claims that places can be physically consumed to a negative end when what "people take to be significant about a place . . . is over time depleted, devoured, or exhausted by use" (Urry 1995:2). Sally Ann Ness argues that tourism, as a form of consumption, "creates non-places," sites that "do not afford experiences of sustainable human relationships and practices . . . [and that are] not available to continuous lived experience" in contrast to "locations where cultural experience can become established and deeply emplaced" (2005:120–21). In contrast to philosophies and theories on the making of space and place, this particular perspective does not allow the touristic consumption of space and place to be socially constructive in any way. As a form of consumption, tourism is thus understood not only to be destructive but also to be completely antithetical to any meaningful cultural experiences, practices, or enduring, significant human relationships.

Representations of past events as displayed through memorial landscapes and in museums are also found to be highly suspect. "In projecting visitors into the past, reality has been replaced with omnipresent simulation and commodification" (Lennon and Foley 2000:78), and this perspective is applied to various types of historical and heritage sites, even those not discussed explicitly as being consumed specifically by tourists. Writing on the process of remaking Hiroshima City and the creation of various monuments and other memorial spaces dedicated to the victims of the nuclear bombing by the United States, Lisa Yoneyama argues that

> through its permanent preservation, the Atom Bomb Dome be-
> came an officially designated site of memory for the collective
> experience of the atom bomb. It will outlive all other atomic
> remains: the hospital wall, the bank building, and many others.
> The dome will then serve like Baudrillard's Disneyland for the
> postnuclear world . . . the neat confinement of atom bomb mem-
> ories . . . obscures one's vision of a world that may be in fact
> thoroughly contaminated by nuclear weaponry. (1994:126–27)

Acts of rebuilding, the installation of memorial architecture, and the creation of memorial museums engender a fear of the erasure of "the real" or at minimum, of a sanitization of the horrific reality of tragic events and their ongoing aftermath. One dimension of this concern relates to the symbolic elements that often make up such sites. Gottdiener, writing on various sites (from the Mall of America to Ellis Island, Disneyland, and the United States Holocaust Memorial Museum), defines such places as "themed" environments in that they are "social spaces in which the public can mingle" where "themed material forms" ("symbolic motifs" deployed in various ways through the materiality of built environments) from and for commercial popular culture dominate (1997:4–5; 2000:270). These sites are considered to represent a sanitized version of reality, because they have been distilled into a system of presumably easily recognized symbols that are also assumed to be closed to polysemic interpretation or contestation. In the case of historical and commemorative sites of or for tragic events, this reductive process of "theming" is understood to result in inauthentic representations of events—a commodification into "unreal" sites that obscure or, even worse, trivialize the awful reality of the past.

Other discussions centered on Holocaust sites provide some insight into why authenticity is seen as so problematic, even more so when tightly linked to such consumptive practices as tourism. Cole finds the production of Holocaust sites for visitation to negatively affect the effective transmission of "real" memory, arguing that this process results in an inauthentic product, a superficial commodity:

Like the survivors, the relics and the ruins of the past will fade away, and then all we are left with is the memory of the "Holocaust" that was created for us, rather than one formed by [us]. All we are left with is a "Holocaust" created for tourist consumption and the end product of "Holocaust tourism." (1999:113)

He finds the ubiquitous presence of Holocaust memorials of all sizes and shapes in cities around the world, most of which are far away from the sites where anything occurred, likewise a means of diminishing the particularity of the tragedy that was and continues to be the Holocaust.[6] Underlying a great deal of Cole's anxiety as well as that of other Holocaust scholars is the fact that at the beginning of the 21st century, Holocaust survivors and witnesses are now passing away. Thus the "possibility of transmitting what one might call 'living memory' [that of living survivors] becomes increasingly precarious," calling into question how we should or even can go about creating and establishing the memory rituals necessary to the ongoing maintenance of Holocaust memories (Landsberg 2004:63–64). But do we, as Cole does, throw our hands in the air in despair over the omnipresence, tourist consumption, and "inauthenticity" of these sites? Are there alternatives to the current ways in which historical, heritage, and memorial sites are produced and constructed so that they may be physically encountered by a broad cross section of a living population through activities such as tourism? Could the cultural and historical patrimony that these sites represent be truly "more authentic"? Can these sites even be visited without being entangled in tourism?

However, none of the scholars discussed here who criticize commemorative sites offer much in the way of constructive alternatives for that which they criticize. They instead constantly invoke the "authentic" and the "past" as though both have an apparent, somehow recoverable ontological reality that can be precisely captured and (re)presented. If sites were indeed left "as is" in their presumably authentic form (if this is even remotely possible), they would not only be unsafe for visitation but would also not be amenable to such in general owing to various safety issues, physical accessibility, and services such as narrative guides, restrooms, and shelter. If sites were left "as is," the artifacts and ruins would surely fade away—it is active preservation that keeps them viable in the present and for the future, even if only for a short future, depending on their material robustness. Without access to sites such as the Holocaust's death camps, we would lack one of the key means for creating and maintaining rich and productive official, public, and vernacular history, powerful memories, and knowledge for future generations. Access to Holocaust sites is critically important, given that there continues to be active denial of the Holocaust, that we are losing living memories of camp survivors, and that new acts of genocide continue.

What, if anything, would then be circulated through society as a means for marking tragic events, making sites and events historically salient, discussing the repercussions of violence, and producing historical knowledge in the present and the future? Television shows, films and movies, magazine articles, or photographic essays? Even worse might be wholesale event simulations in theme parks, museums, or virtual reality venues that are constructed solely as a means to maintain "perfect authenticity" at the original location by isolating it from any physical interaction. This approach would restrict most historically important places to what scholars consider "a still lower circle of tourist hell . . . 'armchair tourism'" (Mintz 2004:185), whereby second- and third-hand encounters with places, cultures, and people could transpire only through visual media consumption, not physical travel and the bodily engagement necessary to powerful prosthetic memory and knowledge.

As part of these and other debates over cultural and historical authenticity, David Lowenthal argues that "the pasts we alter or invent are as prevalent and consequential as those we try to preserve. Indeed, a heritage wholly saved or authentically reproduced is no less transformed that one deliberately manipulated" (2005 [1985]:xviii). The "past reality" that is invoked simply is not "out there, or rather back there. . . . [T]here is only the present, in the context of which the past is continually being recreated" (Urry 1995:6). The fact that few realistic and digestible solutions have been proposed or are ready at hand suggests that perhaps our energy is better spent reassessing some of the dominant assumptions about consumption and commodities in relation to meaning-making that explicitly and implicitly inform so many of the anxieties over the relationships among tourism, commemoration, heritage, memory, and historicity.

CONSUMPTION AS CULTURALLY MEANINGFUL

Consumption is the very arena in which culture is fought over and licked into shape. (Douglas and Isherwood 1996 [1979]:37)

I do not in any way endorse runaway consumption—or over-consumerism as some may call it—but I do recognize that in many societies, consumption and commodification are entangled with literally everything in contemporary everyday life, even that which is believed, somehow, to be absolutely beyond the reach of commodification.[7] Ironically, the deep integration of consumption and everyday life is perhaps most clearly demonstrated in the MasterCard advertisements that tick off a list of costs for multiple tangible items that result in a "priceless" intangible experience or activity (for example, "$60 for baseball game tickets, $15 for hotdogs and peanuts, $10 for a giant foam fan finger . . . an afternoon spent with your son: priceless"). Even though the intent of these ads was to demonstrate that "there are some things money can't buy" and for that which money can buy, "there's MasterCard," the bottom line is that even those "priceless" moments are wrapped up in costs, directly or indirectly. Although an afternoon spent with one's child may not require the high costs of attending a baseball game, simply going to a local park or doing a craft project requires some kind of expenditure in the form of transportation to the park (and perhaps at minimum, taxes paid that maintain the park) or the art supplies needed for making crafts. Under our existing forms of capitalism, there are few, if any, human activities that can be done or objects with use-value produced entirely without the direct or indirect exchange of money.

In the classic economic sense, commodification is the process through which things, as well as activities, operate and become understood in the world in terms of the use-value of the objects or activities plus their exchange value in a monetized, widespread market economy. These objects and activities satisfy some kind of human need (use-value), and they have the power to require other commodities in exchange (exchange-value)—particularly that most highly symbolic of all commodities, money. When the exchange value is of something other than money or other commodities, the objects and activities are construed as "non-commodities" and largely understood, in the Maussian sense, as "gifts." This produces a binary framework of positive/negative meanings and social effects in the world, opposing noncommodities against commodities in the following manner:

noncommodity—commodity
nonmonetary exchange value—economic exchange value
culturally productive—culturally consumptive
authentic—spurious
meaningful—meaningless
positive social effects—negative social effects

The crux of how the meaningfulness of the object or activity is assigned lies in the difference between the production processes of noncommodities and commodities and how their sign (meaning) values are differentially understood.

In this framework, noncommodities, because of their direct and clear connection with human labor as the means of their production, are accorded meaningfulness and authenticity. In contrast, commodities are mysterious, absolutely abstracted from the human labor involved in their production; therefore, any meaning accorded to commodities simply cannot be authentic or socially valuable. Commodities are fetishized objects and activities, carrying sign values that are spurious, because they hide, abstract, and make "magical" the true social conditions of production (Taussig 1997). The consumption of commodities is therefore understood as a form of false consciousness that produces a system of human knowledge based on inauthentic sign values thus having few (if any) truly positive social effects in the world—and, in some cases, even the constructive use-value is of a questionable nature.

A central problem to this framework is the definition of *noncommodity* given the reality, as previously noted, that under capitalism and most forms of modern market economies, the existence of objects and activities that are noncommodities is largely impossible. What, under capitalism, can form a "gift" in the Maussian sense? Yet the insistence that the gift/noncommodity is possible and that it carries a more "pure" sign value and thus meaning continues to inform scholarly frameworks. In his analysis of the similarities between gift and commodity, Arjun

Appadurai argues that the "exaggeration and reification of the contrast between gift and commodity" (1986:11) and the subsequent understanding of the commodity as diametrically opposed to sociality and reciprocality have numerous sources. They include scholars' "tendency to romanticize small-scale societies; conflate use value (in Marx's sense) with *Gemeinschaft* (in Toennie's sense); the tendency to forget that capitalist societies, too, operate according to cultural designs; the proclivity to marginalize and underplay the calculative, impersonal, and self-aggrandizing features of non-capitalist societies" (Appadurai 1986:11). Rather than working to understand how commodities and consumption are indeed possibly meaningful in contemporary everyday life, scholars not only invoke but also idealize a precapitalist age in which objects and activities were not abstracted through commodification.

In this romanticized precapitalist past, there was presumably an absolute "unity between the self and societal institutions, which endowed [this] pre-modern existence with 'reality,'" and tourism scholars in particular consider contemporary tourists to be looking for this "reality" through travel, because it is absent in their own alienated lives (Cohen 1988:374). The contemporary tourist is seen as the "quintessential, if tragic modern person searching for authenticity in an increasingly meaningless world" (Hummon 1988:181), having "been condemned to look elsewhere, everywhere, for his authenticity, to see if he can catch a glimpse of it reflected in the simplicity, poverty, chastity, or purity of others" (MacCannell 1999 [1976]:41). Alienated modern humans are doomed to ceaselessly search beyond their own day-to-day lives, "nostalgically looking for something deeper to fill a meaningful gap in their lives" (Dann and Potter 2001:76). Although scholars—and presumably all alienated modern peoples whether they are conscious of their alienation or not—yearn for this "authentic reality," they cannot generally find it, because even that which is presented as "authentic" in travel is commodified and its sign values manipulated. In the frameworks that guide many scholars of tourism, it is precisely this "artificial" manipulation of the sign and its resultant "inauthenticity" in the form of "superficial and contrived experiences" (Dann and Potter 2001:76) that is so highly problematic.[8] According to G. Llewellyn Watson and Joseph Kopachevsky, the "corrosive power of modern consumerism" renders all tourists' experiences as predetermined, manipulated commodity signs, resulting in the inescapable "ideological domination and alienated leisure" of non-agentic tourist subjects (1994:657).

Watson and Kopachevsky's assertion exemplifies the theoretical and intellectual foundations that inform and authorize Urry's tourist gaze, MacCannell's staged authenticity, Boorstin's pseudo-events, and other canonical theories from tourism studies and beyond. The standardized view of the contemporary tourist as the "quintessential, if tragic modern person searching for authenticity in an increasingly meaningless world" (Hummon 1988:181) is thus the logical outcome of theoretical and intellectual positions that fundamentally view commodities and their consumption as spurious, meaningless aspects of modern human being-ness in the world. And perhaps most interesting, as Cohen so wryly noted, the scholar of tourism appears to be the only person who is immune from the magic of the commodity because "he [sic] is assumed to be able to penetrate beyond appearances, and discover the deception . . . [while] the unsuspecting tourist, who is less sophisticated and knowledgeable than the analyst, is assumed to be taken in by such prevarications" (1988:374).

Given that many historical and commemorative sites would fail to exist without the direct or indirect economic support of tourist visitation—thus requiring some manner of commodification—understanding consumption solely as antithetical to meaningfulness creates a serious contradiction in understanding actual lived social practices under capitalism. In particular it prevents us from understanding how the processes of commemoration and memorialization that are expected to be exempt from the realms of commodification and consumption do occur in these realms with both positive and negative results, not just destructive ones. This perspective also obscures the very real inseparability between the material and the experiential as a significant means through which individuals make sense of their worlds. It mistakes the material world for the individual and societies and in the process, reifies both objects and humans in a manner that I find counter-productive for understanding human meaning-making in modern society. In contrast, understanding consumption as culturally productive engenders insight into how certain forms of consumption can work "to negate the abstract nature of the commodity through rituals of appropriation by which social groups [and thus identities] are created" (Miller 1993:19) and reproduced. This perspective enables a highly needed, more grounded, constructive discourse on consumption and commodification in relation to the performance of human meaning-making activity in general under capitalism and globalization (see, for example, Comaroff and Comaroff 2000).

Ethnographic works by Daniel Miller (1997), Mihaly Csikszentmihalyi and Eugene Rochberg-Halton (1981), and Mary Douglas and Baron Isherwood 1996 [1979]) address such processes of meaning-making through consumption by privileging humans and the material objects/materiality of their lives as the primary subjects of inquiry and analysis rather than societies and commodified objects in the abstract. Although their points of departure and goals for understanding consumption are all quite different, all these scholars regard the consumption of material things—both objects and built environments—to be a significant, central, and constructive part of the human cultural process of making and expressing identity and social relations. Miller (1997) takes a novel perspective on meaning-making from an ethnographic material culture studies approach that diverges productively from what he argues to be the two primary approaches to consumption, commodification, and capitalism: Marxist and post-Marxist economics frameworks and cultural studies analyses.

According to Miller (1997), these approaches reify "society" and the fetishization of commodities through their respective foci on the economic behavior of societies and the decoding of literal texts as well as objects as texts. In such studies consumers are seen as the "end-point" of the "production of commodities, as complex symbolic formations" who "'choose' to accept or reject what commerce has produced" rather than as active participants in the broader social construction of commodities from their inception through consumption and use (Miller 1997:4). Although these approaches have proven useful for numerous intellectual projects, if we are truly concerned with the ways in which humans make selves and social worlds through everyday acts of consumption, such a perspective yields little information about the lived importance and meaningfulness of consumption in contemporary life. To get at the meaningfulness of commodities and consumption in everyday life, we must necessarily move away from the "production-dominated Marxian view of the commodity" and instead focus on its "total trajectory from production, through exchange/distribution, to consumption" (Appadurai 1986:13).

In their ethnographic work on a particular category of commodities, household objects in everyday use, Csikszentmihalyi and Rochberg-Halton draw from the works of Hannah Arendt and Martin Heidegger, positing that "men and women make order in their selves . . . by interacting in the material world"; thus "the things that are around us are inseparable from who we are" (1981:16). Rather than seeing household goods simply as communicating one's social status to others or as purely functional (or highly dysfunctional) objects, they view them as objects that "also make and use their makers and users" (Csikszentmihalyi and Rochberg-Halton 1981:1). Douglas and Isherwood argue that "commodities are good for thinking; [we should] treat them as a nonverbal medium for the creative human faculty" (1996 [1979]:41). As such, commodities are fundamentally communicative objects and activities whose meanings and effects in the world emerge through an ongoing process of semiosis and use (Csikszentmihalyi and Rochberg-Halton 1981). They may be understood as signs that fall into the categories of Peirce's (1940) triad of sign forms (symbols, icons, and indices), and, as with approaches to language in practice, the study of commodities as communicative objects and activities should be investigated ethnographically, focusing on consumption in everyday social practice. It is only through such an approach that consumption and commodities can be understood as something more than superficial, spurious, and socially destructive and unproductive.

Edensor, analyzing tourism at the Taj Mahal, argues that "symbolic sites that engender deep levels of engagement among those for whom the site has national, religious, political importance are so 'full' of meaning that they cannot be rendered superficial through their commodification" (1998:6). Although his argument does not directly challenge the assertion that commodification is solely superficial, Edensor's acknowledgment that such sites as the Taj Mahal, Gettysburg, and Auschwitz are fundamentally symbolic and powerfully important along numerous lines of identity is critically important. These sites are redolent of different and shifting symbolic, iconic, and indexical meanings to different people and communities of belonging, indicating that we should understand travel to such places as socially constructive in terms of processes for identity and historicity-making.

In the case of what has been negatively termed "dark" tourism, understanding travel to commemorative historical sites as socially constructive provides a means for investigation into the diverse ways that physical visitation to sites shapes human imagination and agency in representing, narrating, and apprehending violent events in history. These historical commemorative sites can thus be understood as one of the many material means through which knowledge about and memories of historical events are generated and become a part of individual and collective identities. Like most tourist sites, they are places

> for locating the broad debate over self and society. . . . Tourism is a metaphor for our struggle to make sense of our world within a highly differentiated culture . . . it directs us to sites where people are at work making meaning, situating themselves in relation to public spectacle and making a biography that provides some coherency between self and world. (Neumann 1988:22)

As a part of making (our)selves in the world, contemporary society deals with a "heritage that hurts" (Schofield, Johnson, and Beck 2002:1) through the entanglement, if not the inseparability and artificiality, of the culturally constructed and codified

categories of the "sacred" and "profane" in actual social practice. As a form of consumption, tourism plays a key role in this
grappling with such a "heritage that hurts," because it is through
visitation to commemorative sites that some of the most powerful
physical and emotional engagements with the visual and material
culture of tragic events occur. It is also through this engagement
and the various tourist practices that are performed both on-site
and post-visit that the diverse and dominant meanings accorded
to memorial sites and the events and victims commemorated are
socially constructed over time. It is not simply a matter of "if
and when you build a memorial site, visitors will come"—for
instance, a violent event occurs, a formal memorial is built, and
then tourists consume the site as a part of travel. This position is
one that regards tourists simply as end-point, passive consumers.

   Instead, tourism and its associated social practices play a
part in a far broader, more complex process of commemorative
site-making that, in some cases, begins very shortly after the
occurrence of a violent event of scale (typically in the form of
makeshift, temporary memorials) and proceeds throughout various recovery processes. In the remaining chapters I present a case
study in how tourism and tourist practices play a significant but
largely unacknowledged role in the ongoing social performance
and processual construction of select contemporary commemorative sites even before and while they are in the process of becoming formal memorial places. With a thankful nod to Bruner's
(2005) articulation of what an ethnography of tourism should
look like, I engage in an exercise of taking tourism, tourists as
meaning-making humans, and the objects and places that they
make and that make them very, very seriously.

CHAPTER 5

Marking Memorial Spaces, Making
Dialogic Memoryscapes

Figure 5.1 "Tribute in Light" (© Joy Sather-Wagstaff 2005)

BEING THERE, SEEING THIS THING

In downtown Manhattan, on September 11, 2005, a half dozen young women and men spilled out of the oversized revolving doors of the Millennium Hilton Hotel onto the sidewalk, the women tugging at tiny skirts and purses, chatting loudly about how many cabs they need to get to their destination restaurant in Chelsea. It was unusually quiet outside for this time of day, and people seemed to be moving much slower than usual. Early dusk in Lower Manhattan is normally filled with the sounds of honking cabs, buses, hordes of workers emerging from an after-work drink or late appointment and rushing to the PATH and subway stations across the street, chatting on cell phones. That evening it was just a little quieter, a little less rushed, a little less busy.

These young people quickly noticed that almost everyone within sight was, for the most part, standing still or walking with slow, careful steps as they looked up at the sky. Following the line of vision established by others on the sidewalk, they saw the white beams of the Tribute in Light emerging against the quickly darkening sky, jarring them into stillness and silence. One woman pulled a credit-card-sized camera from her purse, stepped forward, and quickly turned around, snapping a photo of the group as they stared at the beams. "Why'd you go do that?" one of her friends asked. "I wasn't ready!" another complained. The photographer replied, "I've never seen ya'll look so, um, serious."

I was sitting in the sidewalk garden area outside the Millennium, watching and recording peoples' reactions to the lights, jotting down yet more endless notes on the day's encounters, events, and interviews while I could recall them, waiting for it to become just dark enough to get spectacular photographs of the Tribute in Light. The woman who took the group photograph turned and asked me, "What is this? It's not like those movie light things 'cause it's not moving, right?" I told her that it is the Tribute in Light, first lit on March 11, 2002, and then every September 11 since from dusk to dawn and that this year it is located in a different place, south of the World Trade Center site.

That it used to be in a place where you could actually go walk on the lights, an experience one New Yorker said "was like being in heaven." That some people think that the white fragments seen floating and soaring in the lights are the souls of those who died at the WTC, rendered visible to mere mortals for one more night.

I did not stop to think that with today's date—the fourth anniversary of 9/11—that they could have possibly misinterpreted the striking, incredibly predictable iconicity of the towers' recreation in light. They told me that they did not know about the Tribute in Light, only that the site just across the street was an important place to visit and see what remained, a place to remember the victims and that awful day, especially today on the anniversary of the attacks. I understood this much later when reviewing several years' worth of newspapers from around the United States, all dated on or close to the anniversary. This was the first year that media images of the Tribute were truly widespread, appearing on the front pages of even the smallest towns' newspapers. These young people simply did not know—how could they have known what this was if they were not from the region or had other information about the Tribute from the media?

A small group of best friends from high school that take a trip together each year now that they are in college and scattered hundreds of miles across three Southern states, they had come to Manhattan for a minivacation, a way to reconnect and renew their friendships face-to-face. They had indeed been to what they called "Ground Zero," walking the viewing wall just across the street while the official commemorative ceremonies were held below street level at the towers' footprints. They had indeed seen the outpouring of people and grief and left their own mementos, searching the nearby streets for a place to buy a bouquet of roses and lilies to leave on the viewing wall with hastily scrawled messages to the dead and their families on hotel stationery from the Millennium Hotel concierge. And now they took in the blazing white beams cutting into the dark night sky, motionless with awe just like the others who lined the sidewalks—fellow tourists, the hot dog vendors around the corner, a hotel bellhop on break, the local workers ready to call it a day and commute home to New

Jersey, uptown, Brooklyn, Queens, Chelsea. They had now made the place a part of themselves, marking it, seeing it, taking pictures of it, contributing to the collective commemorative display that would be seen by thousands that day and into the night, perhaps even the next day.

Non-locals, like these young people, are often perceived by locals as mere sightseers who are visually consuming what has already been emplaced in this memoryscape and the gaping space where the towers once stood rather than as participating agents in the making of the site. The site is also considered empty—if there is nothing there to visually consume, why visit? A distinctly local perspective, one offered most freely by persons who work and/ or live in the area or who resided in New York at some point in time since the towers were built, is that the site is "empty." They actively retain a memory of the space as full of buildings, workers, vendors, and the bustle of everyday life—an occupied, living place, not a wide open, empty, and seemingly uninhabited space, something atypical of any part of Manhattan perhaps save parts of Central Park on a weekday. To some, there is truly nothing to visually consume compared to the past; for others, there are the flowers, notes, posters, and plaques, all of the materials of an informal memorial but one that should not be tainted by the presence of tourists.

Yet tourists do actually *do* far more than passively sightsee, visually consuming whatever happens to be in the landscape. They explore, experience, and mark their presence in this memoryscape in numerous ways, engaging in performative activities that encompass all the senses, not just vision. The performative activities that mark visitors' presence in commemorative memoryscapes, be they that of the WTC or other sites, include graffiti and other epigraphical forms of literally marking the site, the making of commemorative folk assemblages, the purchase of souvenirs, and taking photographs. These acts of *marking* places and presence are a constitutive part of the process of *making* places historically salient and meaningful both individually and collectively, given that they persist in memory and material form far beyond the performance of the acts themselves.

Commemorative historical places should be understood as constructed through human thought and performative ritualistic activities rather than as "passive receptacle[s]" (Smith 1987:26) of historical importance.

MA(R)KING PLACE I: FOLK EPIGRAPHY

"Eduardo, you have a pen, give me your pen." "Why? What're you going to do?" "Write my name. Right here." (Grandmother to her grandson at the WTC, 2004)

In contemporary usage, the word *graffiti* is typically defined as a criminal or, at the very least, socially inappropriate defacement of a surface that is not the marker's property. At sites of tragedy, violence, death, and remembrance, however, a wide range of popular epigraphical practices are performed, among them graffiti and participatory message-making on surfaces that are provided specifically for such. At the WTC site, the Oklahoma City National Memorial, and many other contemporary commemorative sites, this mode of visual and material expression is a widespread practice, taking numerous material forms and serving multiple communicative and commemorative functions. As discussed further in the next chapter, in Oklahoma City as well as several museum exhibit spaces dedicated to 9/11, writing as a means of leaving one's mark at a site is encouraged, and the process has been highly formalized; at the Oklahoma City National Memorial, specific locations in the museum and the memorial landscape are dedicated to the writing of messages and statements or to leaving temporary artwork.

At the semiformal site of the WTC, this marking has taken a wide number of forms, from the traditional definition of graffiti as a marking directly on a surface in the landscape to the provision of banners and posters by individuals and organizations for public participatory marking. At both the WTC and the Oklahoma City sites, this range of folk epigraphy is a means for speaking to and of the dead and expressing individual and collective sentiments regarding the events and their aftermath in current contexts. This practice is not just a series of embodied acts that literally mark the site but also one that is part of the active process of making the site historically salient in individual and collective memories. Despite the numerous signs formally forbidding graffiti and leaving items at the WTC site (Figure 5.2), visitors write on fences, construction barriers, sidewalks, and scraps of paper, leaving messages to specific victims, a simple "I was here" name and date, sentiments of sympathy, patriotic statements, and political criticisms. Although not all visitors produced graffiti, most took the time to read the writings of others, and graffiti became subjects for photographs and videos. Visitors expressed an understanding that their acts of writing and reading are critically important in the embodied, participatory, and "lived" experience of the tragedy, their visit to the site or sites where events occurred, and the ways in which they will remember both.

Creating graffiti is a highly dialogic practice, a means for "speaking" to anonymous persons who are not copresent, socially positioning both writers and readers and contributing to a wider visual material and embodied discursive field of meaningfulness

Figure 5.2 Port Authority of New York and New Jersey sign on the viewing wall (© Joy Sather-Wagstaff 2003)

accorded the event, the space in which it occurred as a place for commemoration, and the memories lodged in individual and communal historicity. In the public spaces of commemoration these markings constitute a series of "image acts" (Bakewell 1998:22) whereby the text, as a public utterance, is understood as a communicative visual image with the capacity for diverse social actions and effects. An act of display in general "not only shows and speaks, it also does" (Kirshenblatt-Gimblett 1998:128), and graffiti and other forms of folk epigraphy are indeed agentic, conversationally linking writers and readers, producing sometimes profound, powerful, and unexpected social effects. As image acts these temporary markings of grief, empathy, commemoration, anger, cultural criticism, and political sentiment represent both paradigmatic and diverse perspectives in performative public conversation. Contrary to what is often assumed, the WTC site is not wholly dominated by a single political, formal commemorative narrative of victims, heroism, and patriotism. There are instead numerous narratives from visitors that are processually woven between, among, and against the formal plaques and signs narrating the events of 9/11, visitors' spoken and written conversations, and the material culture that make up the ephemeral commemorative folk assemblages on display.

Antiwar and progressive political sentiments act in conversation with jingoistic patriotic discourse, articulating alternative means for "never forgetting" other than through war, political bigotry, and projections of cultural or religious superiority. These sentiments, taken together at any one moment, represent the wide array of meanings, often contestational, for the site. The acts of writing these sentiments in the form of graffiti is socially understood as somewhat less problematic than verbal utterances, since the site is actively policed for what may be construed as offensive, questionable, or "profane" verbally performative behaviors. This occurs through both civilian-to-civilian policing and police department regulation.

During my fieldwork at and around the WTC site, police officers focused on controlling public communication by large, organized groups of protesters, be they victims' family organizations, antiwar demonstrators, demolition and other conspiracy theory groups, or people criticizing the 9/11 Commission's official report. Although allowed to be on the site, protestors' numbers were limited, and the protestors were actively prevented from engaging with passersby through direct, extended conversation. Individual protesters were policed in similar ways, kept at the margins of foot traffic thoroughfares and prevented from forming groups, In general, groups or individuals who actively challenged the official story of 9/11, asserted various government conspiracies, or who disagreed with the LMDC's plans for redevelopment were targeted for the highest level of control at the site; this was particularly so on national holidays, the anniversaries of 9/11, and days with high levels of tourist visitation.

Until construction began again on the WTC PATH station, the open area along Church Street directly outside the station was a common space for group protests following the reopening of the station. Both visiting tourists and commuters from New Jersey and Metro subway riders would pass through this area as they exited the station. On the 2004 anniversary of 9/11 a group from WINGTV (World Independent News Group Television) protested in this space, holding a large banner stating "9-11 World Trade Center Controlled Demolition" while passing out DVDs and printed informational materials in which they claimed that the U.S. government was responsible for the destruction of the towers via controlled demolition.[1] A woman holding a banner and wearing a T-shirt stating "The Revolution Is Being Televised" asked passersby, "How is it possible that they told us everything was vaporized but DNA remained?" Some stopped to argue with her, forming a small, highly agitated cluster of locals and tourists. The argument became heated, and the WINGTV protestor screamed, "I can't believe you people from the boonies believe the crap they feed you!" at two middle-aged tourists who dared challenge her claims. A man dressed head-to-toe in clothing imprinted with the Stars and Stripes and carrying a full-sized flag on a 15-foot pole shook his head and waggled his finger at the group, leaving to pose for tourist and media photos elsewhere.

Heavily armed police suddenly converged on the group and told the WINGTV protestors to keep the sidewalk clear. They were instructed to cease spoken discussion, because it was causing people to stop, and protestors are not allowed to block pedestrian traffic on the sidewalks. The group continued waving the banner and passing out materials in silence, but, frustrated, they left the area completely within 15 minutes.

In contrast, I rarely saw confrontations between persons who were writing graffiti and others who happened to see the act of writing. Witnesses tended to wait until the writing was completed and keep comments, even negative ones, to themselves until after the writer had left the immediate area. When the rare policing did occur as someone marked a surface, communication was immediate and heated, engendering miscommunication, as many confrontational verbal exchanges do. Late one evening on Liberty Street along the south edge of the WTC site, a young man quickly scrawled "Homeland Security = Fourth Reich" on a large banner listing the names of the victims of 9/11. A woman shouted, "Stop! This is not right. It is not about *you*, *this* is about the victims." He did not look at her, but as he walked away he screamed, "No, it IS about ALL OF US!" The woman who had shouted then turned to the man accompanying her and exclaimed, "Ick, 'Fourth Reich'—he must be a Nazi," completely missing the point the man intended by making an image act equating Homeland Security with the information and social control mechanisms of the Nazi government. Later in the evening other visitors expressed offense at his graffiti for a range of reasons; a man from Wisconsin thought it "anti-American," while a young couple from London found it rude to write political statements on "something so beautiful [as the banner] honoring the dead." Others, however, nodded in agreement with his message, a few even adding graffiti about "Adolf Rumsfeld" and the "damnable thought-control machinery" of a "New World Disorder."

Graffiti markings are, however, clearly considered a more acceptable form of both protest and commemoration than are some other verbal and embodied performances. This acceptability is due in part to how the fleeting physical act of writing graffiti renders the message semi-anonymous even despite the frequent inclusion of names and other identification information. Although some encounters between graffiti writers and other people can provoke potentially problematic and violent interactions, as in the case of the "Fourth Reich" graffiti, markings as after-the-fact image acts engender asynchronous dialogue and conversation between persons who may hold vastly differing subject positions. This practice of marking—leaving graffiti as image acts for public display and consumption, however temporary—is a participatory form of expression that has a number of salient social effects.

The first effect is that which results from embodied experience, the act of marking one's physical presence and expressing sentiments (Figures 5.3 and 5.4), tucking the action away

Figures 5.3 and 5.4   Graffiti on the viewing wall
(© Joy Sather-Wagstaff 2003)

in memory, perhaps even photographing it for posterity. The second is that of viewing and reading, being "spoken to" by non-copresent fellow visitors. The act of reading is powerful: one may agree with the content, one may disagree (Figures 5.4 and 5.5), one may find one's subjectivity transformed, one may be moved to tears. Third, taken collectively by the viewer, these image acts constitute a collective reflection on the event itself that changes over time. The conversational component to the graffiti in Figure 5.3 represents two different positions that create, at minimum, three distinct statements for viewers to interpret: "God bless USA," "God help USA," and "God bless help USA."

Likewise, the ongoing conversation in Figure 5.5 is representative of this collective reflection and individual contestation, with the patriotic statement that "these colors don't run" flanking "nationalism kills," "mulims [*sic*] kills" (or is it "nationalism kills mulims [*sic*]"?) and "nationalism kills provides freedom."

Reading graffiti left by loved ones as messages to specific victims often evokes deeply emotional and empathic responses. Judy, a retired administrative assistant from Florida, was taken by surprise at how long she spent reading messages along the WTC site. We first met when she turned and exclaimed to me, "Heavens, I was only going to be here for a half hour but now it is 3 o'clock [2 hours later] and I've lost my companions!" before asking for directions to Wall Street, where she was to meet her friends if they became separated. She then insisted

Figure 5.5　Graffiti in the Liberty walkway
(© Joy Sather-Wagstaff 2003)

that I come and read a particular bit of graffiti that she found most interesting: "I will never forget you Gene Marie. Remember the night before. I will never forget you. Kevin. XX" I saw several of Kevin's messages this particular year (2003) placed in regular intervals along the accessible parts of the viewing wall, and I was deeply touched and profoundly saddened by his words and pain.

Judy told me that Kevin's message was so moving to her because she had lost her husband the year before and frequently wrote little notes to him that she saved in a box. "But," she said, "We knew Conrad was going to die. He had cancer. We knew when he was going to die almost to the day when it happened. You can ask my friends if we can find them. But this Kevin, he had no idea. He had no idea *when* he was going to lose the one *he* loved." Her own loss and grief rituals contextualized how she understood and empathically experienced something akin to the grief felt by Kevin and other family and friends of all those who died at and beyond the WTC on 9/11.

Graffiti is an ephemeral, temporary mode of communication that is understood to have these real social effects; it is usually quickly removed by city and civic organizations as a means to remove "dangerous" or "offensive" images as well as to keep private and public property free of "unwanted" visual clutter. This is also the case at the WTC site; graffiti on construction panels, fences, and sidewalks is heat steamed or sandblasted away, or painted over on a regular basis. However, with visitors persistently leaving marks, some commemorative sites, even temporary ones, anticipate this behavior and provide legitimate surfaces for marking. At the temporary Flight 93 memorial in Pennsylvania, to prevent visitors from marking directly on the property or on other people's messages, blank books and comment cards are provided, all of which are collected by the National Park Service and will become a part of the permanent Flight 93 memorial archive. At the WTC and other temporary sites some visitor markings are actively promoted and archived in highly creative ways by both individuals and various civic organizations not directly involved with oversight of the commemorative sites.

The wide array of formal and informal materials provided for marking sentiments represents an outgrowth of older traditions, such as condolence books at funerals. Influencing and popularizing this new epigraphical tradition even further is the late 20th-century practice of leaving blank, spiral-bound notebooks as part of making commemorative folk assemblages, a custom that Sylvia Grider notes as emerging with the death of Princess Diana in 1997 (2001:2), and at the WTC site an array of marking surfaces can be found. Foam core "memory boards," spiral-bound notebooks, elaborately printed banners, and painted and stretched canvases are provided by individuals and groups, offering a socially sanctioned alternative to the "defacement" of public property and a format for the expression and archiving of public sentiment (Figures 5.6–5.8).

Various individuals and organizations have consistently provided such temporary surfaces for graffiti at the WTC site, particularly during anniversaries and weekends. Preprinted posters, T-shirts, and banner-sized articles listing victims' names, iconic images, and themes of peace or mourning were displayed on the sidewalks and construction barriers around the WTC site. Tourists, victims' family members and friends, locals from all walks of life, survivors, and returned rescue workers made drawings, left messages, and wrote sentiments with the pens, crayons, and markers provided. Some of these canvases and posters for marking are provided by various activist, peace, religious, and youth groups (Figure 5.6), and others from nonprofit and charity groups such as the Save The Cross Foundation (Figure 5.7), family organizations, and ArtAID,[2] and yet others by individuals (Figure 5.8). The completed marked items are intended for display in future formal memorial sites and museums or traveling exhibits, and several of the Hiroshima peace groups have exhibited marked banners from 9/11/03 and 9/11/04 in cities throughout Japan. And for as long as I have been visiting the site a local artist, Edward, has been providing flags and large

Figures 5.6 and 5.7 "Hands Joined" banner and "Save the Cross" poster (© Joy Sather-Wagstaff 2004)

Figure 5.8   Visitors reading and writing on Edward's flag project
(© Joy Sather-Wagstaff 2004)

canvases painted with his own original artwork for visitors to write on, creating a unique archive that combines his art with public participatory expression (Figure 5.8).

MA(R)KING PLACE II: THE MATERIAL CULTURE OF COMMEMORATIVE FOLK ASSEMBLAGES AND SOUVENIRS

Banners, canvases, posters, and flags also form one aspect of a particular type of public, contemporary commemorative folk assemblage of visual and material culture (Figure 5.9) that has become popularized worldwide since the late 1990s. In general terms "folk assemblages" are defined as intentionally arranged formations and displays of material culture that are "created for [viewing by] an undefined public" (Santino 1992:27), by individuals or groups. They are "holistic entities made up of symbolic elements placed in proximity with one another . . . the meanings of each element inform the other metonymically; the assemblage itself is a context that frames each symbolic element within" (Santino 1992:27–28). Examples of assemblages range from secular and religious holiday decorations displayed on home exteriors and in yards to combinations of material culture laden with political symbolism, such as an outdoor fir tree decorated with holiday lights, U.S. flags, and yellow ribbons. Assemblages publicly communicate the subject positions of their makers, be

Figure 5.9 Viewing wall commemorative assemblage
(© Joy Sather-Wagstaff 2007)

they religious (a Nativity crèche and illuminated angels), secular (an inflated Mickey Mouse dressed as Santa Claus and illuminated reindeer), prowar or promilitary (a snowman dressed in fatigues holding a flag next to a tank made of snow), or antiwar, protroops (a hand-painted sign wreathed in yellow ribbons demanding the end of the war).

At and beyond contemporary sites of tragedy and death, both small and large scale, the commemorative folk assemblages that often arise in response to such events are what folklorists term "spontaneous shrines" and the media often calls "makeshift memorials" (Figure 5.9). They are "unmediated folk art" collections of material and visual culture arranged for display as memorial tributes, what Grider considers to be a "tactile and visual expression of our connectedness to one another" during the times of uncertainty and mourning that follow tragedies (2001:1). These assemblages typically appear as close to the site of the event as possible but are not limited to these sites.[3] Following the death of Princess Diana assemblages emerged near the underpass in France where she died, at Buckingham Palace in London, and at British embassies worldwide. Likewise, assemblages for tragedies such as the Challenger space shuttle explosion, the Columbine High School shootings, and the Oklahoma City bombing emerged in numerous locations, many very far away from the site of the actual events.

The media have played a key role in the popularization of commemorative folk assemblages by highlighting them and thus encouraging them as a memorial response. Their now predictable emergence follows each new catastrophe and death. Television news broadcasts and newspaper reports of deaths and other disasters treat these assemblages as primary visual subjects, second only to images of and interviews with grieving family and friends. The practice of leaving items at the Vietnam Veterans Memorial in Washington, D.C., and the ubiquity of photographic images of the Wall decorated with material culture also inform a broader understanding of leaving tributes as a public ritual. The popularity and high visibility of roadside crosses and assemblages dedicated to the victims of car accidents, often the result of drunk driving, have likewise played roles in the spread and exponential growth of public commemorative assemblage practices.[4] These public assemblages commemorate (largely) ordinary people whose deaths were not "good deaths" but ones that were unexpected, disruptive, and violent and that did not allow final farewells—aspects that in the Western world increase the level of tragedy already accorded to death in general.

Despite the inherently temporary nature of these assemblages, they are now an expected public, participatory form of mourning. Efforts to collect these ephemeral assemblages in some form have emerged as organizations such as City Lore in Manhattan and the collecting curators in the Oklahoma City Memorial Museum and the Smithsonian National Museum of American History have acknowledged their value as historically specific, expressive material culture forms.[5] The Oklahoma City Memorial maintains a section of the fence that surrounded the site during recovery and construction; this fence runs along one entrance to the memorial landscape and is covered with assemblage items left by visitors. Such permanent displays of collected assemblages by museums and memorial sites add another dimension to the life span of commemorative assemblages as well as facilitating the circulation of their forms to a public audience that perhaps will in the future engage in similar assemblage-making.

Not unlike religious shrines, these secular assemblages are a means for publicly paying respect to the dead while producing social effects, both individual and collective, including bereavement, participation in imagined communities of belonging, "closure," and spiritual or emotional healing. As Grider notes, the assemblages that emerged around the world following 9/11 as "spontaneous and communal performances of grief" were also a means for "people to work out a personal connection to an otherwise numbing catastrophe" (2001:1). Using Victor Turner's (1974) framework for understanding social dramas, assemblages may be considered a part of the redressive action phase of social dramas, not unlike, as Diana Taylor (2005) argues, the performative aspects of a funeral. During this phase assemblages play a role in containing the social crisis of a tragedy through performative and public rituals of grief, providing a means to enact and perhaps ameliorate the ambivalence and fear that result from a drastic rupture in the social fabric of the "normal" everyday. In addition to these particular functions of commemorative assemblages, the acts of contributing items to these assemblages or engaging with what others have contributed are also a means of marking one's presence at the site and participating in making sites meaningful and sacralized for both selves and others.

Commemorative assemblages appeared around New York City immediately following 9/11, primarily in public locations such as parks and the larger transit stations, because much of Lower Manhattan was largely off- limits during the rescue phase. These sites and their ephemeral contents represented a "noisy democracy," places for grief, protest, affirmation, and solidarity (Haskins and DeRose 2003:383). Similar to the material culture that characterized these and most contemporary commemorative assemblages, the items I observed to be most commonly present in the assemblages at and around the WTC included:

- flowers (single, in bunches, and in complicated arrangements)
- artwork (small- and large-scale drawings, paintings, collages, and three-dimensional items created by children and adults)
- candles (from tea lights to glass-encased, prayer and saint candles and red-white-and-blue pillar candles)
- strings of origami peace cranes
- posters and printed banners from local and non-local communities
- photographs (of victims and of the WTC before 9/11)
- cards (sometimes addressed to specific victims, specific New York fire departments or police units, or the people of the United States or New York)
- T-shirts and hats (often signed, usually from a specific location beyond Manhattan, often from non-local rescue, fire, and police units around the world)

- religious items (crosses, angel dolls, prayer cards, and so on)
- toys (particularly fire trucks, police cars, superhero figurines, and stuffed animals)
- WTC-themed souvenirs
- U.S. flags and flag-themed items and flags from other states in the United States and other nations
- poetry and song lyrics (usually printed and appearing in multiple iterations around the site)
- fabric badges and adhesive stickers from non-local rescue, fire, and police units from around the world

Other items found somewhat less frequently included beverages (a can of soda or six pack of beer, usually accompanied by a note to a specific victim), local and non-local business cards (often with a hand-written message), plastic sandwich bags containing rocks or dirt, food items (such as candy or bread), front pages of newspapers from 9/11, homemade CDs of commemorative songs or hymns, inflated superhero-themed balloons, Mardi Gras beads, and even beautifully crafted mezuzah. These assemblages are a complex combination of secular, religious, and political material culture, and they represent contemporary forms of many older traditions from cultures around the world for remembering, honoring, appeasing, and representing the dead.

As with graffiti and banners, although not every visitor to the WTC site contributes to the making of these assemblages, most do spend time looking very carefully at and physically engaging with assemblage items. Tourists would carefully read cards and messages, smell the flowers, touch stuffed animals, and re-light candles that had flickered out (Figure 5.10). Although it is indeed locals that participate most heavily in the building and temporary maintenance of these assemblages, particularly on holidays and anniversaries, non-local visitors contribute articles much in the same way that they leave graffiti on posts and banners. Even the huge assemblages that immediately emerged after 9/11 in Manhattan but away from the WTC site (such as in Union

Figure 5.10   Reading cards on the viewing wall assemblage
(© Joy Sather-Wagstaff 2004)

Square Park) as well as around the security fence surrounding
the Murrah building in Oklahoma City shortly after the bombing
included direct and indirect participation by non-locals.

In 2002 a Pasco County (Florida) banner (Figure 5.11) hung
on the fence at St. Paul's, representing the communities of Pasco
who sent rescue personnel to New York in late September of
2001 and who engaged in numerous fund-raising programs for
victims' families. Over a period of a few months this banner
went from a fresh, unmarked item to one covered with written
messages and layered with flags, business cards, T-shirts, notes,
and rescue worker patches from various Florida communities.
Through dozens of conversations, I found that most of the tourists who left materials at the Pasco banner either lived in or close
to this particular part of Florida, had relatives who lived there,
or knew rescue workers from Pasco County who volunteered in
New York as part of the rescue and recovery effort.

Figure 5.11   Banner from Pasco County, Florida
(© Joy Sather-Wagstaff 2002)

Tourists also brought other items with them from home that they intended to leave at the site. Among such items were collections of email messages sent by friends, family, and co-workers that had been printed out and condolence cards signed by groups of people that were then carefully attached to the viewing wall or other surfaces at the site (Figure 5.12). Hats, T-shirts, and patches were brought by fire, police, and rescue personnel from around the world and left to mark their presence at the site and express solidarity with those who worked the recovery efforts in Manhattan (Figure 5.13). These practices were performed as a means to "bring" persons who could not, and may never, visit the site in person and to display for a broader public their sentiments of emotional support, grief, and political positions despite geographical distances.

The souvenirs sold at vendor tables around the site also appear in these commemorative assemblages. Visitors who did not bring an item with them often purchased 9/11 commemorabilia such as hats, T-shirts, key chains, postcards, keychain lanyards, toys,

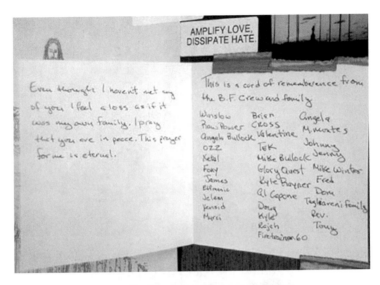

Figures 5.12 and 5.13   Signed card; cap from the Coushatta Tribal
Fire Department (© Joy Sather-Wagstaff 2003)

and photographs in order to participate in assemblage making
(Figure 5.14 and 5.15). They typically personalized the souvenirs with names and various sentiments and then placed the items
at the site, alongside the existing items. Louis, a tourist from
Oregon, did both of these things in 2003, bringing a set of printed

Figures 5.14 and 5.15 Keychain with message; FDNY souvenir
T-shirt (© Joy Sather-Wagstaff 2004)

messages from his publishing company co-workers to leave and
then later purchasing and leaving a personalized souvenir. While
speaking with a street performer, I saw Louis tape the messages
to a construction barrier in the Liberty walkway, leave, and then
return with a Fire Department of New York cap that he signed
and clipped to a lanyard left by another visitor. After he finished,
he asked me to use his camera to take a photo of him next to the
pages he had affixed to the barrier. In explaining the pages he
said that "When people in my office got wind that I was coming
here for some meetings, they got sort of crazy. . . . Kim [his as-
sistant] sent around this email so everyone could sign it, and they
made me bring it here." Louis thought this a little odd at first but
agreed to bring the pages with him even though he did not actually contribute a message.

Once he was at the site, had secured the pages, and spent some
time looking at the other items left in the assemblages in this one
corner of the site, he felt the need to leave something as well.
Louis said that he felt he had to leave "something of quality,
more permanent," and so he purchased the cap from a vendor
and left it in a colorful grouping of caps, badges, and lanyards,
marking proof that he, too, had been there. As for a number of

visitors who did not anticipate seeing the outpouring of emotion that these assemblages represent, it was the physical and emotional experience of seeing what had already been left that motivated Louis to personally participate in this assemblage-making by buying and leaving a tourist souvenir.

Purchasing souvenirs of the trip is another means of marking and making the site through the use of material culture. As discussed in Chapter 4, the numerous vendor tables around the WTC site offer a variety of goods for purchase, and tourists (as well as locals) carefully select the items that will become one of many material representations of their experience. Caps and T-shirts dominate the vendors' merchandise selection, and these typically include items with generic "New York City" themes, NYPD and FDNY logos, and 9/11- or WTC-specific themes, all of which can be found at any souvenir store or vendor table elsewhere in Manhattan. Likewise, the crystal paperweights, key chains, rescue-worker themed toys, 9/11 books, commemorative coins, snow globes, and lanyards that are sold around the site are also sold widely throughout Manhattan. Such items can also be found beyond New York—from truck stops in Nebraska and Illinois to around the world via eBay or the official New York & Co. Tourism Bureau online store. Despite the ubiquity of these mass-produced goods, the act of purchasing these items close to the WTC site endows them with a particular kind of extraordinariness. They are considered distinct from the same merchandise seen at a shop in Times Square because of their proximity to the WTC site; they are understood by tourists to be a *part* of the site itself, and thus when purchased there they acquire an additional aura of meaningfulness and authenticity.

MA(R)KING PLACE III: PHOTOGRAPHY

In addition to the purchase of souvenirs, the tourist consumption of places is considered by some to be "clearest in the stereotypical activity of picture taking" (Gottdiener 2000:269). However, photography is more than just a form of site consumption—it is also critical practice in the ongoing performance and social construction of sites. As a form of site consumption, to photograph what one encounters in the landscape is to capture one's visual, kinesthetic, and emotional experience in a relatively more enduring visual material form. At the WTC site it may have seemed as though there is little to see and photograph given that rebuilding was in process. Although some formal commemorative elements had been established in the landscape, as noted in the Introduction, a Manhattan tour guide claimed in 2004 that there "really isn't much here most days [to take pictures of] until I point something out to them"; then he contradicted himself when he added: "Well, then there's the victims' names [plaques] that they all take pictures of and the flowers." And in the years following, more and more space and pedestrian access around the site have been restricted as construction moves forward.

Yet for tourists at the WTC site, most of whom are seeing the site for the first time, there are many diverse objects and people of photographic interest in what some people consider an "empty" landscape. Visitors, including locals, take photographs of the aforementioned commemorative assemblages, graffiti, and protestors as well as performers, tour guides, the occasional art car, other tourists, construction equipment and laborers, police officers, and firefighters. The most popularly photographed objects at the site during 2003 were "The Cross" (Figure 5.16) and the centermost plaque listing victims' names on the viewing wall (Figure 5.17), with the majority of those I spoke to having photographed both of these items. Until the erection of the viewing wall, the commemorative assemblages that covered the fence at St. Paul's Chapel and views from the temporary viewing platform characterized many tourist photographs. Visitors do, however, carefully pick and choose a diversity of objects in the landscape as photographic subjects.

In 2006 Peter, a firefighter from Canada dressed in his formal uniform, carefully opened his cell phone and took a photo of the FDNY's "The Last Alarm" memorial fire engine parked alongside Liberty Plaza Park (Figure 5.18). At that moment I too was taking photos of the truck, and, noticing this, he looked up at me and smiled, saying, "My [firefighter] brothers [back home]

Figure 5.16   "The Cross" (© Joy Sather-Wagstaff 2003)

Figure 5.17   Viewing wall plaque listing the names of 9/11 victims
(© Joy Sather-Wagstaff 2006)

Figure 5.18 "Last Alarm" memorial fire truck
(© Joy Sather-Wagstaff 2006)

will be so thrilled to see this right now!" Still smiling, he sent the photo while telling me that he and several of the firefighters to whom he was sending the photo had worked in the rescue effort here for a few months in 2001. "This is a big year" he said, noting that "the official firefighters memorial is [now] here" (Figure 5.19), and since he was the only one visiting this year (while on his honeymoon), he had been entrusted to take photos for everyone back at his unit. While he sought out memorial objects and sites at and beyond the WTC that were explicitly dedicated to the FDNY and the sacrifices of firefighters, he said that he had also taken numerous photographs of the commemorative assemblages left on the viewing wall. He found them very moving, much as he had when he was working recovery in 2001, when they could be found throughout Manhattan, and particularly so given that people were still leaving them regularly, something that he had presumed would end rather quickly. Like many others, he also took several photographs of the graffiti and other markings he found particularly interesting, considering them to be a key part of the commemorative landscape and knowing that they, too, were not likely to endure.

Figure 5.19   FDNY Memorial Wall (© Joy Sather-Wagstaff 2007)

In 2006 Jennifer, visiting from California, described posing for a group photo at the viewing wall underneath the plaque of victims' names (Figure 5.17) as different from her pleasure photos in terms of purpose, intent, and meaning. She said that "taking these pictures here [at the WTC] is not like having my picture taken with the Naked Cowboy singer guy in Times Square . . . that was silly, like a tourist . . . it's more like when we went on over to Ellis Island and took pictures of when we looked up family at the center on the computer . . . it's important, historical, . . . really personal." She distinguished between the act of photographing historical sites that were deeply intertwined with her own, very serious personal history and other activities that were novel, fun, and memorable in a far more lighthearted way.

The plaque of names was chosen for her group photo, because, to her, it was the most important formal commemorative object in the landscape. Her familiarity with other memorials of scale, particularly the Vietnam Veteran's Memorial, which she visited the previous summer, shaped this perception. For Jennifer and other tourists anything that even remotely resembled a permanent fixture in the landscape was considered important enough to document, even if only temporary history timelines or printed informational signs. Before visiting, she had few expectations regarding what she would see there, because her local media had not provided much information about the site's development, an experience shared by many non-local visitors. The plaque was also important, because it contained victims' names, a feature that the tourists with whom I spoke considered fundamentally central to any contemporary memorial.

Tourists and local visitors alike also photographed their participation in the commemorative activities discussed in the previous sections, from leaving their own contributions at the viewing wall as part of the daily creation of commemorative assemblages to joining strangers in creating the informal artwork and message banners. Tourists had their companions take photos of them in action as they participated in or took photos of the finished result of the commemorative activity. These "in-action" (but often posed) photographs are, according to visitors, taken in order to document physical presence at the site at a particular moment, as part of creating one's personal historiography of the site. Numerous tourists posed in front of the 2002 Pasco County banner for photographs or had companions take their photos while they wrote on the banner or left an item. Some of these tourists had relatives residing in Pasco County or knew rescue personnel from the area who had participated in recovery efforts, and their intention was to share copies of these photographs with those persons. Other tourists took great pride in having their community recognized so prominently at the site, and they wished to have pictures that not only confirmed their appearance at the site but also provided evidence of the banner in the mass commemorative assemblage engulfing St. Paul's.

In addition, most also feared that the banner would not last at the site, and they felt that a photograph would document its presence for future viewers. They were indeed correct that it would not endure; by the summer of 2003 the viewing wall along Church Street had completely replaced St. Paul's as the locus for commemorative activities and assemblages. With the exception of the appearance of items every anniversary along the Broadway entrance and the remnants of stickers that have resisted complete removal, the fence around St. Paul's is now usually bare. And at the time of this writing in 2009 and 2010 the shifting continues as the viewing fence areas have been replaced with construction barriers and tarps. The loci for commemorative tourist activities are currently at the 9/11 Memorial Preview Site, St. Paul's, St. Peter's to the northeast of the site, the Tribute Center, the FDNY Memorial Wall (Figure 5.17) to the south of the site, and The Sphere in Battery Park.[6]

Tourists also focused their camera lenses on patriotic and pro-war objects such as the elaborately painted memorial art cars, trucks, and motorcycles that frequently visited the site—such as the "911 Tribute to America Truck" (Figures 5.20–5.21). They did so out of curiosity, amazement, and disgust ("I can't be-lieve this guy'll drive this thing around . . . it's tacky, violent, geez, there's the plane hitting the building!") as well as sym-pathy with the sentiments pictorially and textually represented on these highly portable image acts ("Osama's head is in the target right where it belongs" and "Yeah, scumbag terrorists!"). Similarly, tourists and local visitors often took photographs of protesters and performers at the site—from meditating monks, victims' family organization members, and musical performers to peace activists dressed as oversized doves and protestors from 9/11 conspiracy theory groups. Many visitors were astonished to see so much activity at the site, expecting it be a quiet, "politics-free" place, and thus they photographed these unexpected events. Others even posed for photographs with protestors and perform-ers out of support for their cause or out of sheer amusement and basic curiosity at seeing people and activities that were so incred-ibly extraordinary to most non-local persons.

As mentioned, for both tourists and locals, taking photographs is a means of generating proof that they were at the site and

Figure 5.20 Door of the "911 Tribute to America Truck" owned by Anthony Pristera (Florida) showing the Shanksville, Pennsylvania, crash (© Joy Sather-Wagstaff 2003)

Figure 5.21 Makeshift fake missile launcher in a pickup truck bed (© Joy Sather-Wagstaff 2005)

representing what they saw and did there for use in the future as reference to the past. In some cases these photos literally "come back" to the site and are used to craft narratives about the past in the present. In September 2002 I met an ironworker from New Jersey who helped rebuild the World Financial Center's Winter Garden after it was destroyed on 9/11. He told his story to me, a returned Red Cross volunteer, and a sidewalk vendor as he used photos he took during the rebuilding and compared them to photos of the destroyed and completely rebuilt Winter Garden in a book being sold by the vendor. As he gestured to indicate the angle of beams, he pointed to their approximate locations in the various photos. Before leaving us he purchased the book, a rather expensive one, because of the before and after photos it contained. He remarked, with a great sense of pride, that "to see that building [the Winter Garden] on its side, from the air, in color makes me feel like my job [fixing it] was that much more important."

While riding uptown on the subway in 2004 I chatted with two return tourists, Anne and Stephen, who showed me their photos of St. Paul's in 2002. They had just visited the WTC site, and we compared what they saw and photographed during their past and present visits. For both of them the viewing wall simply did not have the same raw emotional impact that they felt when looking at the fence around St. Paul's in 2002. The wall, as Anne said, did let one "get closer to the site [than before], and it's got the names up there, so it's OK, I guess, but there's really not much to it . . . not a lot to look at." While pointing out how sparse the 2004 assemblages looked compared to the masses of material culture on the fence at St. Paul's, Stephen said, "You felt like you had to take your time back then [in 2002], looking through all those layers . . . there was so much . . . yeah, it's more formal now . . . at least you can still leave some things."

Several other return tourists in 2003–2008 also remarked that the site not only looked different but that it also *felt* different; the regular removal of the assemblages, the stark steel fencing, and the historical plaques rendered the site sterile, empty, and far less vibrant than the chaotic, multilayered mélange of new and old objects that once hung on the fence around St. Paul's. To them the viewing wall lacked historical depth and emotional resonance. The assemblages always appeared too recently done, flowers too fresh, cards and posters undamaged by rain and the dirt of the construction site. Yet those who visited in 2007, while the viewing wall began to be covered with construction banners (Figure 5.22), still took photos of the site to mark their presence and what, if only a banner, they had seen. And among the tourists I met who had been to the site more than once since 2001, all referred to their photographs in the narratives of their past experiences as compared to the present. For all who photographed the site, these photos served as enduring evidence—literal markers—of things both material and ephemeral, experiences embodied and emotional, events of terrible violence, different but not wholly unlike the photographs and artifacts displayed in memorial museums and the architecture of commemorative landscapes.

Figure 5.22 Construction fence along Church Street, formerly the viewing wall (© Merlin Hampton 2009)

CHAPTER 6

The Material Culture of Violence and Commemoration in Public Display

Figure 6.1 Statue of Liberty commemorative assemblage,
9/11 exhibit in the New York *USS Intrepid* Museum
(© Joy Sather-Wagstaff 2003)

(RE)COLLECTIONS I

The historical and cultural patrimony of the United States is continually performed through museums, national parks, and memorial monuments as well as family scrapbooks, suburban landscapes, and amateur photos, resulting in a vast cultural topology of collections and displays that span and integrate public and private realms. These geographies of memory, belonging, display, and meaning are, in part, linked in time and space through tourism and tourist practices. Just as visiting a history museum or historical building is a part of making selves as members of communities of belonging, so is visiting a commemorative historical museum or landscape. And as with informal and formal memorial landscapes and commemorative museums already produced for consumption, the continual social construction of these sites transpires through their use: the consumptive and performative acts of tourist visitation.

One of the most frequently asked questions posed to me by tourists in Manhattan was "Where is the [WTC] memorial?" After directing them to the sites that at the time served as memorial spaces, the second question followed along the lines of "So, when will the big memorial be done?" reflecting an expectation that "it should exist and have been completed by now." Formalized sites of scale, like the informal commemorative folk assemblages that emerge following tragic events, are now expected to appear as soon as possible. This expectation is due in part to the proliferation of memorial museums and formal memorial landscapes in the last quarter of the 20th century into the present as public material culture for historicizing various tragedies of the 20th and 21st centuries.

As discussed previously, such sites do not exist in a vacuum outside a wide range of consumptive and performative practices enacted by a broader public. In addition to serving the mourning and memory practices of those most closely affected by such tragedies, memorial sites are consumed by tourists and are a key structure of and for tourism. These sites are physical links to events, places for remembrance as well as for the contestation of official histories through the diverse interpretations of events constructed by individual subjectivities.

This chapter attends to a number of issues with both museums and memorial sites as places of collection—of the material and visual culture of tragedy and of the public—places for recollecting memories and constructing historicities. From the creation of popular symbolic architectural elements and official commemorative narratives and the politics of collection and display to the diverse ways in which visitors personalize these sites and the events memorialized, these places are made, in part, for and by tourists. As with the WTC site-in-process, these formalized sites are made and remade through tourists' and other visitors' entanglements with the material and visual culture of these sites, not just passively consumed. Acknowledging the role of tourists and tourism is particularly relevant given the controversies over what indeed will be included in the memorial museum at the WTC site in Manhattan and the unfortunate fact that tragedies of scale will continue to occur, many of which will result in the creation of commemorative sites. As with the subject of tourism itself, issues over what is appropriate for inclusion in these spaces exist in an uneasy contest for meaning and meaningfulness, fought by differently invested persons and institutions in broad, ever-changing social and cultural contexts that are inextricably embedded in numerous acts of consumption.

PRODUCING AND CONSTRUCTING COMMEMORATIVE PLACES

> Sometimes there are too many words. Too often words turn into attempts to resolve and do not respect the power of events, the power of evil, the power of loss. Silence in terms of the memorial form allows people to fill the voids or empty spaces with what they bring with them. (Linenthal, in Manning 2001)

Commemorative sites are indeed "intimately entangled in such 'profane' enterprises as tourism, economic exchange, and development" (Chidester and Linenthal 1995:1). Given that these sites are often dependent on revenue generated by visitors, either directly or indirectly, and that they might cease to exist without such economic support, this entanglement with consumption deserves more attention than a mere suggestion. Museums, be they art and natural science museums or history and memorial museums, are established by and operate on a wide range on income sources. They may include direct national and local government funding, private and public grants, individual donations and endowments, corporate funds, and visitor-generated income from entrance fees as well as concessions sales and gift shop revenue, particularly for free-admission museums.

For example, the Oklahoma City National Memorial landscape, overseen by the National Parks Service, is free and open to the public 24 hours a day, whereas the Memorial Museum charges an admissions fee. The museum is owned and run by the Oklahoma City National Memorial Foundation, a nonprofit organization, and it receives no federal funds despite being on federal land and an official affiliate of the National Parks Service. To maintain operations the museum thus depends on fund raising, entrance fees, an established endowment, and gift shop revenue as well as proceeds from an annual memorial marathon. And for most museums of scale with admission fees, the two largest proportions of visitor-generated income come from school-age students on field trips and non-local tourists.

The number of visitors to commemorative landscapes and museums is astounding. The *USS Arizona* and the Pearl Harbor Memorial Visitors Center, run by the National Parks Service, have 4,000 visitors per day. Since 1947 over 25 million people have visited Auschwitz-Birkenau in Poland, perhaps the most notorious of the Holocaust death camps. Approximately half a million visitors per year visit the Oklahoma City National Memorial (opened in 2000) and Museum (opened in 2001). Since 1993 over 23 million people have visited the United States Holocaust Memorial Museum in Washington, D.C. Estimates of the possible number of visitors to the National September 11 Memorial and Museum, scheduled to open in 2011 in Manhattan, range from 4 million to 6 million per year.[1]

Although patronage is critical to generating revenue for the operation of some of these sites, it is also foundational to meeting the sites' mission statements as established by the various civil organizations and government agencies that oversee the sites. The Oklahoma City National Memorial Foundation's mission states:

> We come here to remember those who were killed, those who survived, and those changed forever. May all who leave here know the impact of violence. May this memorial offer comfort, strength, peace, hope, and serenity.

The museum as a place to be consumed through visitation is critical to the second part of the mission. Through consuming and engaging with the narrative of the event by means of the museum, the impact of the bombing becomes known to those who were not there as witnesses to it or its aftermath. Likewise, the Flight 93 Memorial's mission statement reads:

> A common field one day, a field of honor forever. May all who visit this place remember the collective acts of courage and sacrifice of the passengers and crew, revere this hallowed ground as the final resting place of those heroes, and reflect on the power of individuals who choose to make a difference.

Visitation to the commemorative landscape is considered a necessary act of witnessing, which will then enable remembrance, reverence, and reflection on the event and its many victims.

The prominence of both stand-alone memorial museums and memorial landscapes of scale in the United States is a result of the roles that museums such as the United States Holocaust Memorial Museum and sites such as the Vietnam Veterans Memorial have had in the creation of a distinctly 20th- and 21st-century culture of remembrance and public history practices. As a specific type of museum dedicated solely to a particular set of events and their aftermaths, the contents and displays in contemporary memorial museums are often quite different from the traditional history museums of the past. As is discussed later in this chapter, the displays are oriented around selective historical narratives that integrate material, visual, and audio-based culture in a highly interactive manner to create an immersive and poly-sensual museum experience, one that is sometimes criticized as "entertainment."

Memorial architecture around the world has also radically transformed over the last half of the 20th century, starting primarily with the building of Maya Lin's Vietnam Veterans Memorial. For the most part, memorial design has shifted from the Classical architectural styles so common to many war memorials, monuments, and government buildings to more abstract forms whose symbolic meaning is often assigned by designers to the materials used in the built environment. In the United States these symbolic meanings center significantly on renewal, reflection, transformation, and resiliency.[2] The Martin Luther King, Jr., Memorial, the Oklahoma City National Memorial, and the WTC and Pentagon memorials share several elements that are both literal and symbolic expressions of acts of reflection. Pools of water and other water features provide reflective surfaces while also symbolizing reflection, serenity, and renewal. Likewise, highly polished stone inscribed with victims' names and other text is utilized as a literal reflective surface and as a material symbolizing reflection on the event and the victims memorialized.

The Oklahoma City Memorial and the rebuilt Murrah Federal campus across the street include landscape elements symbolizing resilience and endurance. The "Survivor Tree," an American elm that survived the Oklahoma City bombing, is included in the Memorial landscape as a symbol of resilience (Figure 6.2), and rocks from the original Murrah Building bedrock grace the landscaping of the new campus, representing endurance. A cutting from the Survivor Tree was used to grow a tree given to the City of New York, representing, as the dedicatory sign notes, the "common bond, resiliency and renewal" shared by NYC and OKC. During the week of the 2006 anniversary of 9/11 this tree was planted in the Living Memorial Grove next to City Hall along with five trees formerly growing in the WTC plaza that survived 9/11. Trees are not only crucial to making these sites "living places" but are also utilized to represent rescue workers (Oklahoma City) and victims (the Flight 93 Memorial) as well as time itself (the Pentagon memorial and the WTC) as seasonal changes in the trees represent the enduring and predictable cycle of time. In Oklahoma City steel chairs represent the 168 bombing victims with each row spatially mapping where they once worked by floor, the chairs placed on the grassy footprint of the now absent Murrah Federal Building. Small chairs represent the children in the Murrah Building childcare center who died, and large chairs represent the adult victims. Similarly, at the Pentagon memorial, benches represent the 184 victims. They are arranged by the age of the victims and placed in different directions to distinguish between those who died on Flight 77 and those who died in the Pentagon.

What we are seeing is a rather rapid codification and repetition of certain materials and form elements used to generate an easily interpreted and uniformly meaningful memorial site, one that requires very little, if any, explanation to visitors. This "ease of interpretation" and the mainstreaming of new landscape

Figure 6.2   Survivor Tree (© Joy Sather-Wagstaff 2002)

forms would be understood by some as a form of *theming*, by Gottdiener's (1997, 2000) definition. Nevertheless, over the course of my research I found few visitors who completely intuited the intended meanings of the landscape elements.[3] Even those people who were made aware of the intended meanings by the guides or signage nonetheless still embellished the symbolism with their own interpretations. For example, the Survivor Tree is clearly marked as a symbol of resilience in the site's brochures and on a plaque at the tree. Yet an overwhelming number of the tourists I spoke with interpreted the tree in other ways even after reading the plaque. The location of the tree, on a small hill overlooking the memorial landscape, dominated these interpretations, with many visitors seeing it as "a sort of guardian," "maybe a sentry" or "like some kind of angel" watching over the landscape rather than as a literal and symbolic survivor.

In addition, the very materials and designs used in memorial landscapes can be, and are, interpreted as evoking highly inappropriate meanings. Such interpretations occur most typically in the design and approval stages, as they did in the case of the Flight 93 National Memorial in Pennsylvania, now a National Parks Service site, which is expected to open in 2011. The original Paul Murdoch Architects (Los Angeles) design contained the "Crescent of Embrace" as the largest landscape feature. This feature was to be a grove of red and sugar maples planted in a crescent form, drawing attention to a naturally occurring circular shape in the landscape where Flight 93 crossed as it hit the ground and came to rest. The open end of the crescent marked the final landing zone, an area denoted in both this and the final design as "Sacred Ground."

When the winning design was announced and the renderings made public in September 2005, outcry quickly arose. The Crescent of Embrace was interpreted by many as the Islamic crescent (owing to the shape and the red color of the trees), and this was considered fundamentally unacceptable for a memorial dedicated to the victims of Islamic terrorists. After conservative bloggers spread this news widely and clergy began making public statements in the media, thousands contacted the National Parks

Service in outrage.⁴ The design was quickly reworked so that the maples now create a complete circle around the largest feature in the memorial, the natural circle in the land now called "The Bowl." The grove of maples was officially renamed the "40 Memorial Grove" for the 40 passengers and crew of Flight 93 who died.

At the WTC site the issue of whether or not the "The Cross" will be included remains contentious for some invested groups (Figure 5.17). A focal fixture in the temporary memorial landscape since 2001, it was removed from its WTC location in October 2006, and it is now located outside St. Peter's just north of the WTC site. Although there are no official plans to include it in the formal WTC memorial landscape proper, several groups are lobbying for its inclusion there or in the future memorial museum at the site. Arguments over its inclusion or exclusion center on the issue of The Cross as a Christian symbol, a symbol that is inappropriate for the WTC site as a secular space dedicated to remembering the lives of people of diverse faiths and belief systems. Yet when The Cross was still at the site, tourists with whom I spoke interpreted it in various ways, not all of them necessarily Christian or even religious.

Some claimed that it evidences the "presence of God," God's power to save "some of the people," or that it represented the sacrifices necessary to any sort of meaningful salvation for victims or forgiveness of the perpetrators. Others mentioned political and ethical connotations ranging from The Cross as a symbol of world peace to a symbol of what many perceive as the "righteousness" of the current war. Some interpret it as a formal monument, finding it to be representative of the victims or the heroism of rescue workers. Others exhibited a nonsectarian spiritual perspective, expressing a fundamental, deep-seated awe of the miraculous as evidenced by those who survived. To one group of self-identified atheist tourists, it was "something like an 'X marks the spot' place, maybe like the real ground zero." The Cross, like other elements in the landscape, can be, and is, interpreted in diverse ways depending on the diverse subject positions of the interpreters.

Should The Cross remain at St. Peter's, the ground of St. Peter's may be interpreted by many visitors as being an official part of the formal memorial landscape despite the fact that it is not such. Such an agentic respatialization of an official commemorative landscape by visitors to incorporate an excluded, religious object occurred frequently with the *Jesus Wept* statue in Oklahoma City (Figure 6.3). The statue is not located on the grounds of the Oklahoma City Memorial but instead is directly across the street from the site, erected by and in front of St. Joseph's Catholic Church. This church was damaged in the 1995 bombing and served as a meaningful commemorative locus while the formal memorial landscape was being completed across the street. In 2002 I spoke with a family who took photographs of this statue. After telling me where they were from (Texas), they self-identified as practicing,

Figure 6.3 *Jesus Wept* (© Joy Sather-Wagstaff 2002)

small-community Catholics. They said that they found this statue important to the site, because to them it represented the "littlest angels" (the children in the childcare center of the Murrah Building who died in the bombing) and because "Jesus was there when it happened" to take away their pain—this is why he wept. Their specific interpretation of this statue not only was rooted in their religiosity but also informed a larger, public discourse on the site as "sacred ground" that is "watched over by angels."[5] This family's beliefs also led them to actively insist that the statue *was* part of the official memorial site despite its placement outside the boundaries of the formal memorial.

Even when words are not literally present—not marked on landscape elements such as plaques or signs—commemorative sites are never truly silent. They contain particular narratives as expressed through their symbolic architectural forms, images, and artifacts; yet these narratives "speak" to individuals in highly different ways. Despite designers' best intentions, commemorative landscape features do not always evoke intended meanings and thus do not convey the dominant narratives that these landscapes are intended to visually and materially represent. Although such a landscape is intended to represent and inspire reflection, it may nonetheless invoke different reactions in visitors—anger, loss, trauma, sadness, resiliency, or hope. Religious meanings may be mapped by viewers onto secular messages, and objects may be completely misread or embellished with additional meanings. And as with the contest of meaning over what these material landscape elements *should mean* or *do mean* and what *should* or *should not* be included in commemorative landscapes, the display of the material culture of tragedy in local and national museums and dedicated stand-alone memorial museums constitutes a similar arena of contested politics, appropriateness, and multiple interpretations.

DISPLAYING DEATH AND DISASTER

Terrence Duffy, writing on museums of human suffering, says that exhibitions on such a topic are "implicitly controversial, since human rights cannot be easily separated from the political domain" (2004:117). In fact, any and all exhibitions focusing on acts of violence that result in human death and suffering are always going to be subject to different and shifting political ideologies, goals, and contexts given that no narrative of history is ever exempt or separable from politicized domains. Commemorative exhibits, be they permanent or temporary, also shift in meaning for the consuming public in ways that may not be anticipated by planners and curators because of changes in broader social contexts that are far beyond their control. As Paul Williams notes, visitors come to memorial museums "with a sense of history . . . personal conscience then becomes the reference point for an (often internal) dialogue with what we physically encounter" (2007:6). For 9/11 exhibits the war in Iraq is one such contributor to these individual-centered shifts in meaning. The National Museum of American History's *September 11: Bearing Witness to History* commemorative exhibit opened in September 2002, before the war. Once the war began in 2003 this exhibit could be interpreted by some members of the public as a political statement justifying or supporting the war rather than providing knowledge as a means for healing and remembering.

All museological narratives are implicitly partial, controversial, and subject to changing interpretive contexts. In memorial museums and temporary exhibitions, these partial narratives are the intended story that results from a very careful selection and display of visual, material, aural, and written culture. However, individual subjectivities enable visitors to such exhibitions to construct their own interpretations and responses, some of which may fill in the gaps of these partial narratives, contest or assign unintended meanings to that which is included, or even reject content outright. Visitors bring with them an abundance of current knowledge in the form of changing political contexts, prosecutorial activities against suspected perpetrators, or other, broadly circulated information that can transform, add to, or question the official but partial narratives produced by museum curators.

The 2002 official Oklahoma City Visitor's Guide has a half-page photo ad for the Oklahoma City Memorial, stating that the

Memorial Museum contains "damaged artifacts and murals in the museum depicting scenes in Oklahoma City immediately following the bombing [of April 19, 1995]." These "murals" are actually enlarged photographs that wrap around and sometimes completely cover many of the walls of the museum. The aftermath of the bombing, living victims, and rescue workers are the dominant visual images on display in these vivid, color photographs. In other rooms multiple television monitors loop video images and newscast footage. These photographic and video images, along with artifacts from the bombing, form the core exhibit features; they are embellished by, rather than secondary to, various written texts, soundtrack overlays of music and oral testimony, interactive oral history kiosks. It is a highly immersive exhibit that guides the visitor through the chronology of the event and its aftermath.

The visual images chosen for display in the Oklahoma City Memorial Museum represent only a tiny fraction of the photographic collection held in the vast and only partially cataloged archive belonging to the museum. Over 500 photographs are used in the exhibit, and they were carefully selected to fit the museum's narrative of the event—healing, resiliency, and terrorism prevention. For example, in the section addressing the trial of Timothy McVeigh, few singular still photographs of McVeigh are shown. One photograph is the most iconic one, having circulated widely in the media; he is shackled, wearing a bright orange prisoner's jumpsuit, and being led out of the courthouse. Limiting images of McVeigh creates a visual lacuna meant to avoid glamorizing his actions and, by extension, those of domestic militia movements while confirming public knowledge regarding which individual was indeed responsible for the bombing. In this case the selectivity of visual and textual information is utilized to "make heroes" of victims and rescue workers. The story told is thus incomplete, a distinctly nonneutral narrative and very careful (re)collection of events. The decision to restrict certain images precludes a more complex understanding of the event while producing an "official" local, state, and national history of the event that "highlights its [more positive] glories" (Zolberg 1998:79) rather than its failures.

According to Alfred Gell (1998) visual images index different meanings for different people, because we, as individuals, engage with images within variable discursive fields of knowledge and experience that are constituted at both the individual level and the societal level in space and time. A lack of images or other forms of visual representation can also index meanings simply because of their very absence. Tourists who had visited Oklahoma City added their own knowledge about McVeigh (as well as Terry Nichols) as they walked through, filling in the gaps that the museum elided. Visitors actively took the dominant visual narrative cues provided (or denied) them, and interviews revealed that they articulate alternate or more complete narratives. My interview with a World War II veterans group illustrates this point. While talking with me one day, a group of veterans from Kansas City carried on an active and highly animated conversation about the bombing and its aftermath in the context of their own experiences with wartime violence. Referring to one photo of McVeigh, they spoke about Nichols's involvement, questioned the motives behind his delayed prosecution, discussed the American militia movements and why no one ever wanted to acknowledge their destructive potential, and argued whether or not McVeigh deserved the death penalty. Filling the gap left for them at the beginning of the exhibition, at a time when terrorism was considered largely as a foreign practice that affects mostly foreign places, they crafted a richer story post-visit to explain to themselves why terrorist acts of a domestically based origin must be prevented. They also explained to me that they completely understood why others can be extremely committed to defending the nation and what it stands for in general—they said that is precisely what they did during World War II. However, Travis, the most outspoken of the group's members, said that one's patriotism, commitment, and love for country should never result in "intentionally killing your *own* people . . . murdering them."

Certain other visual representations are also absent from the museum's displays. For memorial museums, issues of what kinds of material and visual culture of violence are or are not appropriate for display center on taking into account both intended and unintended responses from visitors. There are no images of dead bodies in the Oklahoma City displays, only photographs of those who were injured and survived or whose photographs were taken well before death, long before the bombing.[6] One room, the Gallery of Honor, contains personal photographs of the victims chosen by their families; these are once private mementos that are now displayed in an oval room, each face appearing to gaze outward toward visitors. For many visitors these photographs poignantly represented the tragic loss of "a reality one no longer can touch" (Barthes 1981:87). Others felt as anthropologist Sylvia Grider did, that "as long as the pictures are on view . . . they [the victims] were not completely lost in that terrible explosion" (2001:3). Through the agency of photographic display, the victims live on in memory and this, too, fits Oklahoma National Memorial's overall positive narrative of healing, resiliency, remembering, and transformation.

Standing in for the broken bodies are carefully grouped collections of everyday items recovered from the debris—key chains, watches, broken coffee mugs, and shoes—arranged in separate vitrines in a separate room. The absence of dead bodies in visual images is noticed by some visitors and not by others—the material artifacts were themselves powerful enough. However, there are some images of bloodied survivors—full color for maximum impact, a decision to not obscure the very real presence and shock of the physical damage and bloodiness that resulted from this unexpected attack in the heartland of the country. Yet although the images displayed are testimony to presence of injury and blood, they were carefully chosen to be of persons alive at the time when the photographs were taken—their wounds were not, with the exception of the blood, particularly grisly.

Photographs of the dead are excluded primarily because of their status as legal evidence and secondarily because of the cultural inappropriateness of publicly displaying images of real and violent death despite the pervasiveness of fictionalized or sensational images of death in the mass media. In contrast, at the

United States Holocaust Memorial Museum, displaying images of the dead was considered absolutely necessary to fully "contextualizing the horror"—the bodies are incontrovertible evidence of the horrors and scale of the Holocaust that works against those who deny that it happened—and the main issue over where they should be located (Linenthal 1995:194). Temporal closeness or distance to the violent event also plays a central role in whether or not images of the dead are included in displays. There is not only less of a chance that the dead bodies shown in the Holocaust Museum's images are individually identifiable— in part because of the condition of the bodies, the quality and composition of the photographs, the absence of clothing—but also because many Holocaust survivors and witnesses are now elderly or have passed away. The exclusion of images of the dead in Oklahoma City thus also demonstrates a concern for the possible trauma such display could cause family members and those close to the victims. A glimpse of hair, jewelry, or item of clothing could identify a victim to a familiar viewer. The emotional impact on others—decades into the future—is unlikely to wane, evidenced by the powerful responses to photographs experienced by visitors to Holocaust museums over half a century after the liberation of the death camps.

Like photographs of the dead, the display of other material culture left after violent events is a highly sensitive issue. What is appropriate to show, and what might be too traumatic an object for viewing? With these questions in mind, one must also consider the desired effect—and the use of "difficult" artifacts is one means for effecting "prosthetic memories" (Landsberg 2004:2) of events for those who were not first-hand witnesses. In 2003 the USS Intrepid hosted a temporary exhibit on 9/11, and one of the main features was a fuselage section of American Airlines Flight 11, the plane that struck the north tower of the WTC (Figure 6.4).[7] The section was housed in a vitrine, surrounded by a layer of ash and paper debris from the WTC site post-collapse. Although the identifying card noted it as the "window/fuselage" of the plane, even from quite a distance it was clearly a plane window, and this drew me and other viewers toward the artifact.

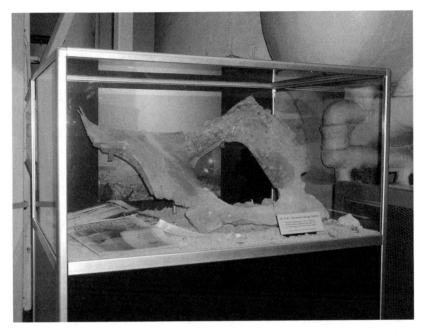

Figure 6.4   Window/fuselage section from Flight 11 in the *USS Intrepid* Museum (© Joy Sather-Wagstaff 2003)

Several tourists I spoke with at the WTC site had visited the *Intrepid*, and their responses to the artifact varied widely. One tourist thought it to be a really important part of the exhibit, because it was a surviving part of one of the planes; like many, he had thought that the planes had been completely vaporized.

But several tourists were extremely disturbed by the artifact, finding it, in the words of a woman from Chicago, "like you're looking at it and someone dead is looking back out the window." A man from Los Angeles commented that he was going to have a hard time flying back to California; he imagined himself behind the window when looking at the artifact. The ability to imagine a victim—or in some cases, even themselves—behind the window made some tourists feel extremely uncomfortable, but they still found it to be something "important to look at . . . it's more real than the TV was," said one tourist. Viewing and interpreting the difficult artifact from their own subjectivities enabled a visceral, deeply felt, prosthetic form of reliving the event and, in the process, making new memories of the event in the present. Similar WTC artifacts have appeared in other 9/11 commemorative exhibits. In the Smithsonian National Museum of American History's exhibit *September 11: Bearing Witness to History*, a twisted portion of a steel I-beam from the WTC was positioned precisely so that it could be touched by visitors, yet few did during my visit. Some expressed a sense of awe when looking at it, but they seemed uncomfortable physically engaging with something that may have indeed been a direct a part of a person's death. A local young man accompanied by family visiting from Texas remarked that the apparent invitation to touch the beam and its location at the edge of a large collection of commemorative objects seemed "really morbid . . . it's OK to see but why [is it] so close to us?"

Issues of how best to present the events of 9/11 through material, visual, and aural culture in the future WTC memorial museum have undergone significant discussion. Central to this discussion are distinctions about the appropriateness of certain artifacts and display methods. In 2005 programming workshops that facilitated discussion on how to most appropriately and effectively present the events of 9/11 focused on two distinctly different possible trajectories for the exhibit spaces, and they also discussed the possibility of presenting both as separate paths through the museum. The first path was envisioned as an immersive "you were there" experience that would utilize intense audio and video records of the events, one that would aim to make visitors feel as though they were in the towers during the attack. This path would include artifacts but focus primarily on the video footage and audio tracks, some of which would include the voice messages left by victims and cell phone calls from the airplanes. The second path was conceived as a non-immersive traditional presentation that would use less intense images, artifacts, and text to tell the story in a more distinctly linear fashion. The 2005 focus groups agreed on the immersive option, with some participants noting that the events should not be "'sanitized' or 'sugarcoated'"—that an intense presentation would be "a way to 'stun' people and 'avoid complacency'" (Civic Alliance 2005:4–5). However, it was also agreed that having two distinct paths through the museum should be considered.

The Oklahoma City Museum includes a specific reenactment as part of their immersive experience. This reenactment occurs at the beginning of a chronologically ordered, linear exhibit organized into "chapters" narrating/describing the bombing, the rescue and recovery process, the trial of McVeigh, the 168 victims, the building of the Memorial, the emotional aftermath of the event, and the diverse local, national, and international responses to the bombing. The exhibit begins with two sections located in a hall: "Background on Terrorism" and "History of the Site." To access the exhibit's main spaces one must go into a separate, closed room at the end of the hall for the chapter titled "A Hearing," which auditorily replays and sensorily interprets the very moment of the bombing as it occurred at 9:01 A.M. on April 19, 1995.

To gain access to this section, visitors wait at the closed door. Once eight or nine visitors have gathered, a museum docent leads them into a room furnished with a conference table and chairs. The door is closed, and the visitors sit on benches along the room's perimeter. The only auditory record of the bombing, the taped minutes of a 9:00 A.M. Water Board hearing that took place across the street from the Murrah Building, begins to play. The names of those present at this hearing are read off, and then suddenly a massive explosion is heard; the exhibit room's lights flicker off, and a plexiglass window on the wall lights up, flashing photographs of the 168 victims. The sounds of car alarms and then police and fire truck sirens follow. At the opposite end of the room from the entrance door, a second door automatically opens, allowing visitors to walk into the first main exhibit space in the museum as the sounds of wailing rescue sirens continue and the news broadcasts reporting the bombing begin.

The first time I went through "The Hearing," my reaction was that this reenactment could very well be viewed as entertainment rather than education, a theme-park simulation not unlike those imagined by cultural critics as discussed in previous chapters.

Undoubtedly some scholars would argue that this is indeed entertainment and thus not an appropriate form for engendering any deeply meaningful, albeit second-hand, witnessing of the event. Yet the creators of this room clearly intended to provide visitors with a small dose of what the event felt like—something totally unexpected, jarring, and painful to witness aurally, visually, and emotionally. Persons I spoke with who had visited the museum did indeed have this reaction, some even swearing that the room physically shook; a few were so upset by what they felt that they needed to leave the exhibit quickly. The use of the only record of the event was meant to provide realism, the most singular and emotionally powerful experience possible, despite the exhibit being a recreation. Most visitors I spoke with understood and experienced "The Hearing" as a forcefully polysensory exhibit.

MA(R)KING PLACE IN THE MUSEUM

Two characteristics shared by the Oklahoma City National Memorial Museum and various 9/11 exhibitions, along with other formal and informal sites dedicated to tragic loss of life, are the opportunity for visitors to physically leave their mark and the subsequent collection and display of these marks by the museums. The type of graffiti and the provision of "proper" marking surfaces that can be archived have been normalized as a social practice in the formal spaces of memorial museums and temporary exhibits, building on the vernacular acts that take place at the original informal, makeshift memorials. Visitors to the Oklahoma City National Memorial are invited to leave messages or drawings in three approved spaces. The first space is a children's area in front of the museum's main entrance, a brick patio that is surrounded by ceramic tiles made by children from around the world and is equipped with sidewalk chalk. The second and third spaces are inside the museum, in the last rooms of the narrative exhibit space. One room is a children's room with print resources and drawing materials, including a computer with a drawing program. Until 2004, when a computer-based system was installed, there was a second room where visitors used dry-erase markers on removable magnetic whiteboard tiles to leave messages on the Wall of Hope (Figure 6.5). [8] Each morning the archive staff removed the marked tiles, photocopied or photographed each tile, erased the marking, and replaced the blank tiles on the wall for the new day's visitors. In 2003 the museum published a book, *Shared Voices: 04.19.95–09.11.01*, containing a selection of the messages left on the Wall of Hope in the months after 9/11.

A number of 9/11 exhibits also include spaces for leaving messages and drawings or for sharing one's own 9/11 experience story. Although some are digitally based, like those at a New York Historical Society exhibit that provided computer stations linked to the September 11 Digital Archive, others provide manual marking options as well. The Smithsonian's exhibit, *September 11: Bearing Witness to History,* included a large room supplied with tables, pens, and paper forms for leaving comments, stories, drawings, and messages. As visitors completed their messages,

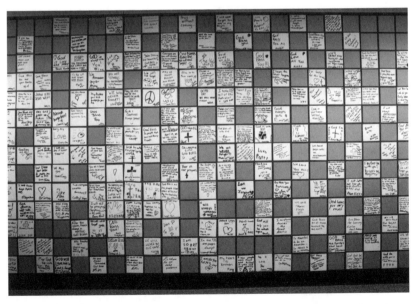

Figure 6.5   The Wall of Hope in the Oklahoma City National Memorial Museum (Ferguson-Watkins Collection, Oklahoma City National Memorial Museum, © Oklahoma City National Memorial Foundation 2001)

they would sometimes even photograph them to remind them of what they wrote and where they were at that moment. Selected forms were pinned to a board at the exit from the exhibit, providing a ready-made display and, like the informal graffiti at WTC site, a meaningful conversation between visitors over time. More than 20,000 of these completed and scanned forms are now available for viewing online as part of the September 11 Digital Archive.[9]

Although the archiving and dissemination of these messages through the internet and print publications do geographically disperse experiences and sentiments that build site meanings, additional social consumption, performance, and construction of commemorative sites also take place post-visit in tourists' communities of belonging. The next chapter deals with the embodied and performative experiences of travel that are continually re-performed by tourists post-visit through stories and the use of the visual and material culture of travel. Tourists return to everyday local spaces, providing sites for research into these post-travel narratives and uses of photographs and souvenirs, the visual and material culture of travel. Attention to the post-travel activities of tourists enables an understanding of how the WTC site as well as historicity about the event and the ongoing aftermath of 9/11 is processually constructed and (re)produced over time and in geographically dispersed places.

The Social Life of Things: Material and Visual Culture of Travel and Personal Historiography

Considering the frequency of commemorative ceremonies and historical festivals, the output of historical films and novels, the number of visitors to historic sites and museums, the intensity of campaigns to mark and preserve historic buildings, or the sales of software for probing family history and genealogy, it appears that if Americans do not have a strong sense of history, they certainly spend a lot of their leisure time looking for one, in historical pursuits of one kind or another. (Glassberg 2001:6)

Memories . . . Memories . . .
Who has the best memory?
Let's find out.
Gather your friends together for a lot of fun and put them to the test.
(blurb from the top of the box containing Snapshot [The Parker Brothers Photographic Memory Game, ca. 1972]

PERSONAL HISTORIOGRAPHERS OF THE (EXTRA)ORDINARY

The performance of ongoing discourses about the place-based experience and the social circulation of images and memories of the experience are key to the construction of 9/11 historicity not only for returned tourists but also for members of their various communities of belonging who may never physically visit the site. Given that *being there* is only part of the meaning-making process, understanding the ongoing process requires the scholar to get "off-site" to investigate the cultures of collecting, narrative, and personal historiography that tourists participate in when living in the post-travel everyday. Through post-visit embodied performances over time and space tourists are re-imagining and re-presenting the events and aftermath of 9/11 and the WTC site in a new context of having borne physical witness to the site, constituting a wider geography of memories and site meanings that is anchored in multiple localities well beyond the WTC site.

Material and visual culture are devices for memory and identity representation, narration, performance, and reenactment in public spaces (be they formal or informally dedicated places to specific episodes in time) and in tourists' post-visit domestic and work spaces. Acts of collection and the display of the material and visual culture of travel in these private and semiprivate places are influenced by and also influence practices of collection and display in public spaces. The private and semiprivate realms of house and workspace and the public spaces dedicated to events and actions from the far and near past share a museological sensibility enacted through the collection and display of material and visual culture. The people of the United States are, for better or worse, a nation of collectors (Rosenzweig and Thelen 1998). As historian John Gillis aptly notes, we seem to have an increasing amount of memorywork to perform, and "every attic is an archive, every living room a museum" (1994:14).

The documentary culture of travel forms a central category for many of these personal archives. Photographs and souvenirs from trips accompany and embellish more everyday material culture collections and displays, provoking narratives, reverie, and serving as tacit physical evidence of sites seen and experienced for both selves and others. From oral conversations to written travel diaries and scrapbooks, narratives of travel experiences are performed as an ongoing dialogue with sites seen and experienced and as a form of storytelling. They enable the sharing of knowledge with those who have not, and may never, visit these sites. They also enable the tourist to revisit and reinterpret the travel experience. Such narratives and material culture thus play performative roles in processually constructing and maintaining memories of travel within changing social and political post-visit contexts. In turn, this ongoing performance of experience and memories works to construct localized subjectivities and the meanings accorded to places seen that are now geographically distant, even for those who have not traveled or may never travel to such places.

A creative and museological sensibility characterizes the ver-nacular material culture of contemporary tourism as it is collected, displayed, and actively used by tourists for meaning-making in the everyday, post-travel. As photographers and souvenir collec-tors, tourists see themselves as personal historians, and this is one of many aspects of contemporary social practices for recording everyday, intimate life with family, friends, and numerous com-munities of belonging. The display and circulation of the ma-terial and visual culture of travel as well as that of the everyday are a means of "making special" (Dissanayake 1990:95), crafting creative display assemblages in the home and everyday semi-public places (such as workspaces) that communicate special and significant experiences to others and reiterate them for us. Our photographs hang on walls and refrigerators, decorate our of-fices, are carefully placed into scrapbooks, and circulate virtually by email, social networking sites, and photo-sharing websites. Our souvenirs inhabit shelves and cubbyholes, decorate tables and desks, and are worn and carried, intended to be noticed and admired by others and to affirm our own sense of self. Indeed, such ritualistic, communicative displays give order to our worlds by creating visual narratives of selves. The collection, archiving, and display of travel souvenirs and photographs are thus a part of constructing identities and subjectivities, aspects of the self that are both made through and represented to others by these mater-ial and visual objects.

The "imagining of possibilities for the self materialized and made tangible through objects" (Hooper-Greenhill 2000:9) and, likewise, the visual and material culture of travel are a means for continually making and remaking the meanings of sites experienced and seen from spatial and temporal distances. Tourists' collection, display, and circulation of the material and visual culture of travel thus play a role in the dynamic and dialogic construction of and contestations among official, public, and private/vernacular/local memories and historicities.

DOCUMENTING TRAVEL: PHOTOGRAPHS OF PLACES AND FACES

I have pictures of my son on the top of the World Trade Center with the flag flowing in the background. That was in May, before the tragedy. My son was smiling and soaking up the awesomeness of the buildings that his grandfather helped to build. Now when we go back, and we have been back four times since, our pictures are much more somber. (Visitor from Virginia, 2003)

In continuing my conversations with tourists once they left the WTC site, I was able to investigate the means through which tourists' photographs perform as the core material and visual artifacts in the post-visit social construction and performance of memories, identities, and place meanings. The post-visit experience is rarely addressed in any depth in studies of tourism or commemorative historical sites, because seldom do scholars continue their engagement beyond a given site. I am especially concerned with photography, and I argue that the cliché of positing a Disneyfication of human experience through photography or other forms of touristic consumption precludes deeper scholarly investigation into understanding the meaningful roles that photographic images play in the everyday.

Susan Sontag's acclaimed *On Photography* (1977) drew critical attention to the power and paradoxes of the social practice of photography as something far more than a mundane practice with few social effects. Sontag addresses the photographic ethics and the moral propriety of photographing violence or representations of violence, regarding the act of photographing as a form of "complicity with whatever makes the subject matter interesting, worth photographing," and such complicity is considered particularly acute when it is the pain or suffering of others that is found interesting (1977:12). This complicity, along with the reproduction and broad dissemination of such photographs, is argued to "goad conscience" but "never be ethical or political knowledge," because "after repeated exposure . . . it [the photographed] becomes less real" (Sontag 1977:20, 23–24). Yet in use, photographs can make the subject matter even more real, establishing "evidence for historical occurrences" and "political significance," even in an age characterized by both mechanical reproduction (Benjamin 1968:226) and digital hyper-reproduction.

Tourists photographing the landscape at the WTC site are presumed to be and are represented as consuming a spectacle, complicit in the pain of others and the corruption of the site—taking photographs "for fun" at a place of mass death and making it "less real." In numerous conversations with fellow academics, friends, and local New Yorkers, I have noted that assertions that this photographic behavior is indeed inappropriate are frequently defended with claims that people do not take photographs at other, similar places, such as the Holocaust death camps and the Vietnam Veterans Memorial. However, the fact is that tourists *do* take photographs at these sites. How can we begin to understand why and how these photographs are used after the visit and what are some of the salient social effects of such use?

Jack Kugelmass's 1994 essay on Holocaust tourism as a ritual form includes photographs of Jewish Canadian visitors to Auschwitz-Birkenau and Treblinka taking photographs of the sites, posing with one another and displaying the Canadian flag. These images figure prominently as accompanying visuals but are not mentioned in Kugelmass's otherwise rich discussion of the rituals involved in travel to these sites and the role of tourism in maintaining deeply intertwined secular and religious identities and historicity in the Jewish diaspora. The photographs taken by these visitors are an enduring material representation of what Kugelmass describes in his text—a deeply meaningful pilgrimage to a sacralized place where participation in rituals that mark membership in particular religious communities of identity are tightly linked to national identities. These photographs are likely to be treasured, shared, displayed, and narrated time and time again, re-performing the powerful experience of having been to the death camps. Yet this aspect of the travel ritual is not frequently addressed as part of an everyday, post-travel realm of identity and meaning-making rituals.

During visits to Washington, D.C., I observed visitors to the Vietnam Veterans Memorial taking photographs of a wide variety of activities, scenes, and objects in the landscape. After having located a soldier's name on the wall, visitors would ask one of the National Parks Services guides to make a rubbing of the name or to provide them the materials for doing so. This is also now a practice at the FDNY Memorial Wall at the WTC, where visitors make rubbings of names or parts of the three-dimensional artwork that constitutes the rest of the memorial wall. At the Vietnam Veteran's Memorial, some visitors also photographically captured the very act of making rubbings of a name. After asking me to take a photo of him making rubbing of the name of a family friend, a visitor from California explained that "taking the picture proves I did it . . . yeah, I could've just ordered a rubbing off the internet but this is the real thing . . . I did it *here.*" His photograph became evidence of the specific, first-hand authenticity of his experience making the rubbing, thus constructing the rubbing itself as more valuable as an artifact of the site in terms of his personal relationship to the site and his memories of being at the site.

Visitors also photographed their children and grandchildren posing at the Vietnam Veteran's Memorial wall while pointing to the name of a relative or family friend, while others asked the guide who helped them make a rubbing to pose for a similar photograph. These photographs were intended for scrapbooks, mantels, and walls, to be shared electronically with family members and friends close to those visiting and who knew the people memorialized at the site. The experiences of seeing, being, and doing there, as discussed in Chapter 5, are considered important as a photographic subject, a making of a material record of the experiential moment as a means to recollect it in the future and proof of visiting the site as "having really happened" and thus having been authentically experienced first hand. The photographs that tourists take at the WTC site serve as evidence of fleeting but deeply meaningful experiential moments, and they act as post-visit historical documents of presence and participation.

Our understanding of why tourists take pictures at these sorrowful sites, what they photograph, how these images are used, and what social effects result from these practices are limited owing to a general scarcity of ethnographic work on tourist photography from a tourist perspective. Few scholars address what tourists actually photograph, and even fewer investigate how individuals put travel photographs into social use post-visit in the service of memory, self, and place-making, just as they do other, more everyday photographic images. A majority of existing works on photography focus on the photographic object itself rather than its use after its making.[1] Works that focus on tourist landscapes and media posit that particular views (sights of sites) and photographs taken of these views are overwhelmingly pre-scripted for tourists through such media as magazines, travel brochures, postcards, television, and other people's travel photographs (see Albers and James 1988; Crawshaw and Urry 1997; Hammond 2001; Urry 2002). Little agency is accorded the tourist/photographer as a photograph maker or an interpreter of images.

Although not explicitly ethnographic, works on the history of photography and travel (Osborne 2000), on family-centered photographic practices in the home and during travel (Bouquet 2000; Chalfen 1987; Haldrup and Larsen 2003; Hirsch 1997; Larsen 2005), and more generally, on photographs as historically specific modes of knowledge production and polysensual historical records (Edwards 2006; Lury 1998) speak more saliently to why we take and use photographs. Photographs are devices for the performance of subjectivities, for the making of various social relationships and cultural realities, and, most important, for memory, recalling the past in service to the present. Tourists' production and use of visual media are thus best understood as forms of "practice rather then representation, as taking part in the world rather than reflecting it" (Crang 1997:360), thus as processes of continually making individual and collective worlds of meaningfulness.

In contemporary U.S. society photographs are indeed used as a significant technology for memory and identity making, particularly when "the object of collective and quasi-ceremonial contemplation" (Bourdieu 1990:26) is in the realm of family and other everyday domains. These domestic domains constitute what Richard Chalfen (1987) identifies as "Kodak culture," a "home mode" of photographic production, consumption, and often highly ritualized performance. Family photograph collections, be they in albums, scrapbooks, filed boxes, or organized computer files, are the locus for these objects and a framework for shared and individual contemplation. These archives are inventories of "identity-yielding events" such as weddings, secular and religious festivities, holidays, and the mundane everyday, which, when in production and use, construct and reinforce memory, selfhood, family, community, and thus identity (Bauman 1996:18). Photographs are powerful communicative technologies for constructing identities and subjectivities that bridge the individual, experiential, and private realms with collective, public ones through the acts of display and circulation (Chalfen 1987; Hirsch 1997; Sturken 1999).

ON THE AGENCY OF DISPLAY: PHOTOGRAPHS AND SOUVENIRS

As a means for the "dissemination of place" in the processual making of places and selves (Coleman and Crang 2002:11), tourist photographs and souvenirs are the key visual and material culture of travel deployed in processes of recollecting and socially circulating memories and narratives of the visit experience after the return home. Ethnographic engagement off-site requires "following" tourists to their communities of residence and creating sustained interactions with them as they continue to engage with their material visual culture of travel. Although post-visit engagement would traditionally require physical mobility on the part of the ethnographer, internet communication technologies and questionnaires can be adapted as means to "purposively create the occasions for contacts that might well be as mobile, diffuse, and episodic as the processes" (Amit 2000:15) we study, creating opportunities for sustained engagements and data collection.

At the end of some of the longer conversations with tourists in Manhattan, I offered a self-administered questionnaire to be completed once visitors returned home. (See the Appendix for the complete questionnaire.) This questionnaire addressed photographic and souvenir collection practices, both in general and specifically regarding the particular visit to New York City.[2] In terms of gathering information on tourists' experiences specifically at the WTC site, one section requested a narrative describing three photographs of the site that they found most meaningful, and another asked questions about where and how tourists displayed their WTC photos. In 2004, 125 questionnaires were given out and 76 were completed and returned by mail.[3] In addition, 31 of the questionnaire respondents and over 36 additional tourists to whom I gave only my address (no questionnaire) self-initiated correspondence with me post-visit. Some respondents sent me invitations to view online photo albums dedicated to their New York trip; others sent CDs or printed copies of photographs; and several simply sent friendly greetings and invited further communication.

In many of these cases we indeed established ongoing communication by email and letters, some of which continues. This ongoing contact engendered numerous opportunities not only for discussing their visit and photographs but also for getting to know one another in more everyday and intimate ways, sharing life events, mundane experiences, jokes—narratives of our selves and subjectivities as we present them to others in the everyday. Although these exchanges were enacted through the internet and letters rather than in person, we cultivated the kinds of sustained personal relationships expected of extended face-to-face ethnographic engagement, thus both upholding and challenging normative ideas about ethnographic research methods.

Through these exchanges we performed narratives emerging from our experiences at and photographs of the WTC site, engaging in what Bruner describes as "tellings and readings" that

> always involve active selves engaged in an interpretive process, selves that are historically positioned in a given time, place, and social situation. But while the meaning of the story is dependent upon these very contextual variables, the telling of the story can also create its own context. The story itself, even if referred to indirectly, may evoke its own mental images, associations, and feeling tone for a particular teller or reader, and thus at least contribute to the construction of the context. (1984:5–6)

Although some consider picture-taking at "dark sites" such as the WTC a form of crass consumption or a morally questionable activity, serious attention to the social life of photographs post-visit and the "tellings and readings" that accompany them revealed something quite different.

One of the most poignant outcomes of these off-site narrative exchanges reveals how tourists' emotional responses to their photographs changed their perceptions about the politics of the events and ongoing aftermath of 9/11. Heteropathic memory evocation, as a form of meaningful and transformative self-identification with that which is otherwise distant geographically or temporally (Hirsch 1997), characterized many of the transformative effects of photograph use post-visit by participants. Heteropathic memory is the result of viewer putting themselves in the place of the person in the photograph, feeling that "it could have been me" or someone else near and dear to the photograph viewer (Hirsch 1997). Such was the case with Sheryl, one of the questionnaire respondents with whom I communicated for an extended period of time after her return home.

I first met Sheryl on September 11, 2004, while participating in the informal part of the annual commemoration rituals enacted by the general public along the viewing wall while the official ceremony took place on the other side of the wall, at the footprints of the towers. As the names of the dead were read over the loudspeakers, "Philip Haentzler . . . Nizam Hafiz . . . Mohammed Hamdani . . ." the woman standing next to me suddenly gasped and turned to me, saying: "Those aren't the names of those terrorists, are they? They can't do that! They can't do that!" I assured her that these were the names of victims who had worked in the towers or were rescue workers, pointing up to the large plaque of names directly above us. She quickly scanned to the letter "h" and became visibly comforted that the names she heard were of "heroes" and not, in her words, "those heathens."

Calmer now, she continued to read the names, no longer really listening to the list being read over the loudspeakers that lined the sidewalk. She turned to me and said: "I didn't realize that there were so many, you know, foreign names, where were these people from? I mean, yeah, I'm from Ohio. Where were these people from?" We began discussing how international New York City is, that it was her first time here, how she knew "from *Law and Order*" about the city and that people from all over the world lived here but not that so many "foreigners" died on 9/11. She asked me where the memorial was, and I explained to her that for now, it was this fence and the plaques and that it would be many years before the memorial and first buildings were completed. She wanted to know more about all this, and I wanted to know more about her. We crossed the street and sat down on the steps in front of the Brooks Brothers store and she asked me when the new viewing wall went up.

I started to answer, but she interrupted me to tell me where she was when it all happened: "I was at the beauty salon, getting a perm like I do every three months—like clockwork or I look like a wet dog! Watching the TV up there best I could . . . and then, oh, it was just terrible and I kept telling her [the hairdresser] to stop [rolling her hair], stop, turn the damn sound on," because something clearly awful was on the news. She recalled the replaying of the plane hitting and the towers falling. At that point her husband, who had left before I met her to fetch a cup of coffee from Burger King, spied us on the stairs, and, being a bit worried that she was sitting with a stranger in New York City, he hurriedly crossed the street to meet us.

She asked if I would take some photos of the two of them in front of the viewing wall, taking the time to choose a location that had a large assemblage of flowers and posters. I did so, and then she took photos of some of the posters and flowers as well as a picture with me. I gave her a questionnaire to take home, and then we exchanged email addresses. I promised to contact her in a few months, and she promised to return the questionnaire. Through the series of emails and letters that we exchanged over the next year, Sheryl created and performed a narrative of self-transformation that resulted from her visit, her engagement with her photographs after the visit, and a new awareness of changing political contexts.

Once a staunch supporter of U.S. military actions in the Middle East, she continually rethought and problematized her position on the war as she experienced heteropathic memory construction while preparing photos for her scrapbook. The photos that affected her in this way were the ones I saw her take at the WTC site—those of the commemorative assemblages, many of which included memorial posters and flyers that featured photographs of victims, often representing happy moments such as weddings or graduations. In her first letter to me, she wrote that when she looked at the photograph she took of a homemade poster commemorating a victim, one of her most meaningful photographs according to her questionnaire, the "whole war business" felt "personal . . . looking at this happy young man's face makes me regret the costs we are all paying now."

In a series of email exchanges we discussed what she meant by this, and she explained that the victim in this photograph-of-a-photograph looked remarkably like her best friend's son, a 25-year-old U.S. Army reservist recently deployed on active duty. Commenting on the increasing human costs of the war "on both sides" and imagining her friend losing a son, she reflected that "if he dies it will not fix anything." Her response demonstrates how photographs characterize a Bahktinian intertextuality in that "it is impossible to avoid encountering the discourse previously held upon the object [photograph]" (Todorov 1984:62), and it is also impossible to obscure current discourses and the new contexts that continue to surround photographs as they are put into social use after their creation. Whereas Sheryl once perceived the WTC site as a place that represented justification for war, she now advocated it as place that should negate violence, one where commemoration should enable positive remembrance, not more war. She shared her new perspective with her local communities of belonging, playing a role in how persons in her communities who had not visited the WTC site came to witness it second hand, primarily through her photographs. She gave a presentation to a local women's book group meeting, passing around and discussing the newly completed scrapbook dedicated to her entire New York trip. She continues to display photographs and souvenirs both in her home and in the suburban elementary school classroom where she teaches.

Like several other participants, she also framed a copy of her photograph of The Cross and presented it to her church, where it is now on display in her congregation's social hall. In all these multiple contexts, her photographs, like those of other tourists, serve as visual representations of sights seen and experienced for others. They are, perhaps more importantly, also a means for engaging in the ongoing making of selves and subjectivities through the narrative performances that accompany photograph viewing. In Sheryl's case her newfound perspective on the WTC as a site for commemoration and peace was shared with her friends and students as they talked about the photographs and her experiences at the site, and she noted proudly in a letter that she had indeed "changed some minds, maybe for the better."

The ways in which Sheryl primarily engaged with and circulated her photos required material photographs even though the images were taken with a digital camera. Although digital photography has ushered in an age of online photo-sharing through virtual scrapbooks, email, and social networking sites, a majority of the tourists in my research accorded primacy to the printed, material photograph for use in the everyday. Even those who used digital cameras would often have a majority of their photos printed for use in the everyday. They value the highly social and tactile qualities of photographs that invite touching, being passed around, and stimulating shared narratives. It is not just the "image qua image that is the focus of contemplation, evocation, and memory" but rather that the image's "material forms, enhanced by its presentational forms, are central to its function as a socially salient object" (Edwards 1999:222).

According to my questionnaire respondents, scrapbooks are one of the most popular presentational forms used for displaying and sharing photographs. A majority of participants noted that at least one person in their household, usually female, engaged in scrapbooking activities.[4] Often elaborately crafted, filled with souvenir objects in addition to photographs, and containing descriptive textual narratives, these contemporary versions of the photographic family album represent a highly expressive form of personal historiography. As with the vacation slideshows of the not-so-distant past, scrapbooks are actively shared with friends and family at gatherings, and they provide yet another social context for sharing travel experiences. These scrapbooks, along with photographs and souvenirs displayed in homes, workspaces, and semipublic social spaces, serve as visual and material prompts for performing narratives about the place-based experience.

As with some tourist photography, souvenirs are interpreted by scholars as having vastly different social value and meanings. Although some consider souvenirs, as vernacular material culture, to be critical to memory, nostalgia, and remembering in the everyday, not simply passive artifacts (Edensor 2002; Stewart 1984), others argue that "the travel souvenir can never be adequate to the experience . . . [it is] an appendage of a modern experience that is devalued" (Leslie 1999:115). It is the latter perspective that places souvenirs in the realm of having questionable meanings and, in the case of commemorabilia available at sites of tragedy, being socially deceptive, engendering "the consumption of mourning and kitschification of grief" (Sturken 2007:130). In terms of deception, this "comfort culture" results in a distancing from the social, political, and economic causes of these tragedies and their aftermaths and an identification as innocent citizens (Sturken 2007). Although this distancing may be the case for some individuals, it is not overwhelmingly so.

Souvenirs do serve as a material connection to specific places and experiences regardless of what forms they take. They do not have to literally represent the site visited, although they often do in some manner. In addition, not all souvenirs or commemorabilia are necessarily related to tourism; individuals' collections might also include objects whose origins are from instances of business travel, special events, anniversaries, and birthdays, or "just because." Like photographs, they are one of the ways in which travel experiences are "infused into the everyday" (Franklin 2003:2), made meaningful over time, and shared with other members of communities of belonging, from family and friends to co-workers. As do many photograph-based scrapbooks, return tourists' scrapbooks frequently juxtapose souvenir objects with photographs as a form of folk assemblages intended for private or semipublic consumption and performance.

Sonny, a tourist from Mississippi, remarked to me that the most meaningful photograph he took (out of 40 or so) in Manhattan was of the memorial inside Engine 10 and Ladder 10 Firehouse, noting on his questionnaire, "all hands [on duty were] lost from that station" (Figure 7.1). He framed a print, and it now sits on a shelf in his office flanked by a toy fire truck and 9/11 baseball cap that he bought from a vendor on Church Street close to the WTC site. A school counselor, Sonny sometimes uses this assemblage when meeting with students, particularly those who are working through loss and grief, as a means to engender empathy that in his words, "helps them realize they are not alone . . . others mourn, too, feel desperate, like the world has ended." Other times he finds that students will ask him about the site, prompted by the display, and this provides an opportunity for him to perform narratives of his experiences there, providing first-hand knowledge about the site as it was to those who may never see it.

Some tourists are highly particular about what constitutes a truly meaningful souvenir. I met Daniel, an avid coin collector, across from the WTC site. He repeatedly remarked that the items we saw for sale at the vendor tables were "all trash, cheap." These

Figure 7.1   FDNY Engine 10 and Ladder 10 memorial inside the firehouse (© Joy Sather-Wagstaff 2005)

items included the various caps, T-shirts, crystal paperweights, books, photographs, and key chains that characterized most vendors' merchandise. He was particularly critical of how everything was "so 9/11." I asked Daniel if he usually buys souvenirs when traveling, and he replied that he did, but only coins and cookbooks. Everything else was usually too "cheap and tacky . . . not attractive or useful." His standards for truly meaningful, authentic souvenirs had to do with not being "tacky," their literal utility after the travel event (cookbooks, preferably for regional food specialties), and his individual sense of aesthetic values (coins) as well as monetary value.

I offered to show him where he might find a coin of interest to purchase as a New York souvenir. We walked up to Liberty

Plaza Park where the usual souvenir vendors were interspersed with coin and baseball card vendors. At the first table he spied the perfect coin, a gold, half-dollar-sized WTC commemorative coin. Interestingly, it had "9/11" on both sides, but Daniel considered this to be okay, "not tacky like those [9/11] key chains back there." I asked him if he would be willing to take home a questionnaire and perhaps converse with me through email about how he displayed his travel souvenir coins once home. He agreed, and several months later, I learned that he kept them in glass-covered, wood display boxes, 15 coins to a box and displayed in numerous spaces.

Daniel's most recent acquisitions were displayed in a box that hung on his office wall, and as new ones were added, the oldest coins were moved into boxes at home. The boxes he kept at his residence were arranged alphabetically by city, state, or country (in that order of priority, depending on which of these identifiers appeared on the coin), and they lined a hallway wall.[5] Daniel traveled alone frequently, usually three or four trips a month for business. Whenever he returned from a place he had not previously visited, his co-workers would stop in his office to look at the new coin and hear about where it was obtained, stories about what he did on the trip, what interesting people he met or places he visited.

He said that the WTC coin "was a hit . . . but it was the first time I ever made anyone cry when talking about my trip." A self-identified Republican and supporter of the war, he told his co-workers that his experience at the site was powerful, that the outpouring of sadness he saw in the assemblages there strengthened his convictions that justice was being done through the war. Despite this, seeing the site made him more sensitive to how many people were still grieving the dead, and he connected this to the immense grief felt by those who were losing family members in the war. "This," he wrote in an email message, "made some people very sad."

As indicated by my "intervention" helping Daniel find an acceptable souvenir coin, I could not avoid becoming part of other tourists' travel narratives and memory-making processes on-site and off-site. Numerous participants asked me to pose with them for photos, resulting in my appearance in several scrapbooks and many a story being told to others of "that anthropologist lady" met while in New York City. Some sent me copies of the photographs they took of me standing or sitting with them in Liberty Plaza Park or Battery Park. And I shared some of my own photos with participants after they returned to their communities of residence, further contributing to their photographic and narrative archives.

On the evening of September 11, 2005, Beatriz approached me as I took photographs of the Tribute in Light, the memorial light sculpture that represents the twin towers every anniversary from dusk to dawn. She asked me if I could help her configure her digital camera to take a photo of the beams, because she did not know how to set it for low-light photos. Being unfamiliar with any camera other than my own, especially the tiny digital cameras, I was of no help. Since we could not remedy the problem, I asked her if she would like me to send her one of my photographs once she got home. Delighted, she said yes, and we exchanged email addresses. I sent the image as promised, and a few weeks later Beatriz emailed me a photo of my photograph, framed and hanging in her family room, not unlike how the same image hangs in my home amid my most meaningful fieldwork and travel photographs, linking my homespace and her homespace with the commemorative place that is the WTC site.

(RE)COLLECTIONS II

Pictures taken and souvenirs collected during travel inhabit multiple spaces and serve as material and visual culture that "make special" the experiences, lives, memories, and identities of those who collect, display, and use this visual and material culture. They evoke both narratives about place and experiences as a part of performing both selves and places in time and space. They are "retained and cherished because of their extraordinary status and their implications for self-definition" (Morgan and Pritchard 2005:32). The collection and display of the material and visual culture of travel constitute a part of the dynamic interactions between dialogic construction of and contestations among official, public, and private/vernacular/local memory and historicity. The material and visual culture of travel plays a key role in personal historiography, and, in the case of travel to commemorative and other historical sites, this historiography engenders a place-based "sense of history" that is

> akin to what environmental psychologists describe as a sense of place . . . locatedness and belonging. A sense of history locates us in space, with knowledge that helps us gain a sense of where we are . . . [it] locates us in time, with knowledge that helps us gain a sense of when we are . . . [it] locates us in society, with knowledge that helps us gain a sense of with whom we belong, connecting our personal experiences and memories with those of a larger community, region, and nation. (Glassberg 2001:7)

The material and visual culture of travel come not only to represent place but also to act as memory aids, allowing us to re-perform place processually as contexts change and time passes.

The ongoing narratives performed through my conversations with participants revealed the ways in which tourists' on-site experiences are indeed remembered in dialogue with present contexts through engagement with photographs and souvenirs, constructing new contexts of meaningfulness not only for the WTC site but also for the ongoing aftermath of the events of 9/11. These performances, in turn, work to socially construct the meaningfulness of the site not only for tourists but also for others in their communities of belonging who have not been to the site. Travel experiences and their associated practices are indeed ways for marking and making places, "leaving our presence in and on the indifferent surfaces of the world" (Osborne 2000: 187), and through these practices, we, too, become marked and transformed by places.

CHAPTER 8

Conclusion: The Contest of Meaning and Cultures of Commemoration

Figure 8.1   Banner at the WTC site for the fifth-anniversary photographic exhibit on the viewing wall: "Here: Remembering 9/11" (© Joy Sather-Wagstaff 2006)

CONTESTS OF MEANING

On September 9, 2006, I returned to New York for my yearly anniversary visit. This year was particularly important, because it was the fifth anniversary of the attacks. I noticed an unusually large number of young people milling about in my hotel lobby and on the sidewalk outside. They appeared to know one another, blending themselves into small groups that stayed together and then separated again, whereas most tour groups of size tend to cluster together tightly in hotel lobbies. What was even more unusual was that these people were almost all male, and all were wearing similar black T-shirts illustrated with 9/11 iconography. Once I arrived at the WTC site, I learned that they were representatives of the 9/11 Truth Movement from around the country. They were here planning to stage the largest protest at the WTC to date, calling for transparency regarding the events of 9/11, citing conspiracy, and requiring an end to the national and global inequality and political power struggles that they believe enabled this tragedy.[1]

On September 11, 2006, hundreds of them filled the sidewalks from the WTC site down to the newly remodeled Liberty Plaza Park, now renamed Zuccotti Park (Figure 8.2). At the official protest area in front of the transit station, several held banners and handed out materials. Although most were mostly silent, several older members actively engaged passersby in heated discussions. Tourists, locals, and members of other protest groups entered into many lively and heated political conversations—many more than I had ever seen at the site. Debates erupted over the Patriot Act, presidential sex lives, the ongoing politics of voting problems from 2004, Homeland "(In)Security," and prowar, antiwar, and

Figure 8.2   Protesters taking a break at Zuccotti (formerly Liberty Park) (© Joy Sather-Wagstaff 2006)

9/11 demolition conspiracy theories. Later that night, back at my hotel, the Truth Movement protestors gathered in a sizable group on the sidewalk. In a truly *Fight Club* (1999) moment, one said to the others, "Let's go, soldiers!" and they walked off together, out for an evening on the town after a hard day spreading their gospel. They had indeed changed, for better or worse, the character of the site greatly with their presence that day.

Protests have occurred regularly at and around the site with various victims' family organizations holding rallies, rescue workers protesting poor treatment for health issues, conspiracy theory groups handing out materials, and antiwar groups staging activities. Yet in 2005 and 2006, as the war in Iraq continued, rebuilding at the site appeared slow, and the formal memorial was yet to be built. Organized public protests escalated in size and regularity; however, in 2007, they began to wane as pedestrian access became limited owing to construction. These protests have been one of many aspects of the contest of meaning at the WTC site, and their presence has also significantly contributed to the experiences non-locals have had at the site. But protestors have not been the only contestants in the struggle for meaning-making regarding the WTC site and the tragedy of the 9/11 attacks as well as the events initiated in the aftermath, such as the war in Iraq.

CONCLUSION: CULTURES OF COMMEMORATION

Violent acts and various natural disasters of scale continue into the present, and unfortunately there is no clear amelioration for either, given ongoing human frailty and the persistence of seemingly insatiable appetites for power, control, and resources. The aftermath of 9/11 alone continues with more terrorist attacks, trials and executions, torture, war, and increasing death counts on all sides. The multiple ways in which the victims of 9/11 and its aftermath, along with numerous other tragedies small and large, are being informally and formally memorialized are contributing to a new culture of commemoration that incorporates old traditions with new ones and that is in many ways radically challenging the distinctions scholars and public historians make between history, memory, and practices of commemoration.

The Many Narratives of 9/11

The narratives in this book contribute to an ongoing "history in the making" that comprises the events and aftermath of 9/11. Although a necessarily small selection, these narratives from both tourists and locals tell us much about the diverse responses to and makings of multiple, vernacular and public histories as they derive from, contest, and inform official histories. The narratives come from the everyday lives of a geographically dispersed public, a public that is engaging with official histories of events and sites while bringing with them their own histories. And in the process they are performing as participants in making commemorative sites such as the WTC site deeply meaningful in many different ways.

The many stories of survivors, victims' families, and local New Yorkers have been told and continue to be told in many places and in many formats, constituting a significant part of the larger series of histories of 9/11. Setha Low argues that although they are important stories and perspectives, they have been largely excluded from corporate discourses on rebuilding the WTC site, because they represent a "diversity of needs and reactions" that do not fit the "official" global meanings intended for the site (2004:331). This limiting of the site largely to its social production is considered by Low (2002, 2004) to be highly problematic. Yet these stories will likely be included in future, broader historiographies of the site as scholars and public historians continue to investigate and include them in discussions on the social production and construction of commemorative sites, much as Low is doing for the WTC site and Linenthal has done for the Oklahoma City National Memorial and the United States Holocaust Museum. My focus has been, instead, on a broad, non-local but highly invested public through ethnographic research with tourists visiting or who have visited these sites.

As representatives of part of the general public that commemorative sites are intended to serve, tourists are a particularly important segment of the population to address, yet they have been largely excluded from study. Perspectives on the WTC as a tourist site see tourism as redefining the site as primarily commercial rather than commemorative. Yet as Marita Sturken observed, tourists have "responded [to 9/11 at the WTC site] in ways that evoked both mourning and tourism—they looked shocked, they cried, they took photographs of what they saw" (2004:317), a reaction also enacted by many local visitors to the site whom I encountered daily. These lived experiences of tourists are all too often denied a role in legitimate public responses of grief and mourning, the writing of histories, and the making of memory. However, the tourists' stories, responses, and perspectives are important as yet another part of the broader public and individual histories and memories that rub up against, shape, and are shaped by official histories and memories as they continue to be made. From Sheryl's personal transformation from prowar to antiwar, to the graffiti image acts on the viewing wall and Edward's collectivist artwork archives of visitors' sentiments, the tourists who have engaged with the WTC site form part of the broader responses to 9/11 and its official histories. Tourists do indeed play a role in the making and remaking of site meanings over time and in geographically dispersed spaces, spaces that constitute diverse, local, lived communities of belonging and broader, imagined communities of belonging.

Tourism and Commemorative Historical Sites

Official commemorative sites, both landscapes and museums, have only recently become a more common subject for research, and, although we know much more about the content and programming at such places, our understanding of a general public's actual engagement with such sites is still thin. Much of this is due to the newness of many of these sites and thus the lack of opportunity to perform in-depth ethnographic research over time at such places. In the process of doing my research on public

engagement with commemorative sites, I have identified a critical contest of meaning indicating a need for future work along a
line of inquiry and public anthropological practice that incorporates continuing to work with tourists (as representative of a general public) as they engage with a site or sites and disseminating
results of this work (and past work) with organizations that are
involved in the production of such sites. This particular contest
of meaning involves ongoing struggles with both defining and
trying to separate "history" from "memory" and "commemoration." This contest of meaning is evident in public talks on the
planning of the WTC museum's programming and content (as
briefly discussed in Chapter 6) given by Alice Greenwald, who
joined the WTC Memorial Foundation as director of the National
September 11 Memorial Museum in April 2006. In one talk she
addressed how the combination of museum and memorial landscape at the WTC is intended to create two separate spaces for
two separate purposes: one for the presentation of history and the
other a place for commemoration (Crapanzano 2007).

My research suggests that in practice, the two purposes proposed by Greenwald are inseparable, because the general public,
victims' family members, and survivors engage with commemorative landscapes *and* memorial museums as both commemorative and historical. Attempts to cleanly separate the two WTC
spaces by meaning and purpose may work in theory but is im-
probable in terms of how individuals are likely to engage with
the completed WTC site. Although the families and friends of
victims will be coming to intimately mourn specific persons,
some will engage in mourning not only at the memorial landscape
(the intended place for commemoration) but also in the museum.
Likewise, whereas the rest of the visiting population may not be
mourning specific victims, they will be engaging in the commemoration of victims both in the museum and the memorial spaces.
And as is clear from my research participants' responses to both
the 9/11 exhibits and the Oklahoma City museum, the intended
meanings of spaces, displays, and narratives are not always consumed and interpreted as such by visitors—visitors' wide range
of individual subjectivities shape their individual interpretive

contexts in practice, and this process is beyond the absolute control of designers and curators.

The persons invested in the WTC site's meanings are many, and the general public is indeed among such invested persons. They have been coming to the site in the millions for almost a decade as tourists; they are contributing donations to the building of the memorial and museum; and they will likely visit in even larger numbers once the memorial and museum are built. Yet although visitors from across the United States and the world are indeed significant as visiting population, they may unfortunately continue to be viewed by locals and scholars alike as problematic for the site in terms of "proper behavior" and maintaining the official meanings and purposes of the site. Those who are not family of victims should not be understood simply as "tourists" at the site who will disrupt or destroy the sanctity of the site. To consider them "casual," noninvested patrons not only evokes Lennon and Foley's hierarchical model of "dark tourists" versus "serious visitors" but, worse, I posit, also scripts the general public as a population that plays no role in generating the many meanings the site holds and will hold in the future. The persistent devaluation of tourists as meaning-makers indicates that in my future work I must continually revisit the issue that I argue underlies the distinctions and paradigms about tourists and tourism: the scholarly and intellectual perspectives that view consumption as destructive rather than socially constructive in any manner.

New Cultures of Commemoration: Transformations of the Vernacular into the Official

Through sustained focus on the WTC site as it evolves and investigating new memorials that emerge, I continue to trace the innovative ways in which contemporary vernacular memorializing acts emerge and selectively become integrated into formal, official commemorative practices. For example, the folk assemblages constructed at commemorative sites of scale and various epigraphical practices of commemoration have clearly become popularized to the extent that they are now expected responses to both small and large tragedies. They are so highly popularized that they can, in some contexts, be perceived as negative rather than positive forms of commemoration. In June 2007 the city of Cleveland, Ohio, considered banning informal commemorative assemblages at fatal shooting sites in certain impoverished neighborhoods, claiming that they worked only to glorify criminal actions. The public outrage, from across the city, over this attempt—for reasons that range from accusations of racism to assertions that these assemblages are critical for healing and the prevention of future criminal actions—caused the city council to rethink passing this ban.

Because of their vernacular nature, these assemblages are also sometimes seen as aesthetically displeasing, and spaces for their placement may not be included in memorial designs. Yet, as discussed in Chapters 5 and 6, these practices are also now emerging regularly as standard components in formal memorial museums and sites in the form of approved spaces for leaving objects and written sentiments. Workshop participants and exhibit planners in New York have unanimously agreed that a crucial section of the future WTC memorial museum will be a reflection room where visitors can leave written messages and commemorative objects. But will there be an official space outside the museum for assemblages like the fence in Oklahoma City, or will such assemblages be discouraged as a means to maintain the sparse, angular aesthetic of absence intended by Arad and Walker in their design? Visitors do continue to leave graffiti and objects around accessible areas of the WTC site, particularly at the FDNY Memorial Wall. It will be highly interesting to see if and how both tourists and locals create ways to maintain assemblage-making at the future, formalized site once it is completed.[2]

The folk epigraphy that marks commemorative landscapes in many forms and is present in memorial museums is also becoming codified as an official, formal practice in a new form: in memorial architecture itself. In March 2007 the newest memorial to victims of the aftermath of 9/11, the M11 Memorial, was unveiled in Madrid. Designed by FAM Studio Madrid this

memorial to the 191 victims of the March 11, 2004, train bombings is a stark but elegant cylindrical tower of glass bricks that
acts as a skylight into an underground space at the Atocha station,
the final destination for the four trains that were bombed. The key
element in this design is the incorporation of commemorative
folk epigraphy: messages selected from those that visitors left
around the site on paper and on computer terminals at the station
after the bombing are incorporated into the interior of the tower
(Figure 8.3). These messages and the sunlight that illuminates the
underground viewing area form the focal themes of the memorial
design, elements that represent sorrow and renewal, respectively.
Of interest is the fact that the original design did not include the
names of the bombing victims, a codified element of most contemporary memorials. Their names were added to the plans at the
insistence of Spain's Association of Victims of Terrorism.

Although this is the first memorial of scale to incorporate folk
epigraphy into the formal memorial design, it will not be the only
one to do so. Folk epigraphy will also be a structural part of the

Figure 8.3   Epigraphy on the interior of the M11 memorial in
Madrid, Spain (© Maria de los Angeles Alfonseca-Cubero 2007)

WTC site memorial. On September 10, 2007, the Tour for the National September 11 Memorial and Museum began in Columbia, South Carolina. The four-month fund-raising tour and memorial exhibit visited a significant part of the U.S. heartland, stopping in North Carolina, Virginia, Pennsylvania, West Virginia, Ohio, Kentucky, Indiana, Michigan, Illinois, Wisconsin, South Dakota, Iowa, Nebraska, Kansas, Missouri, Arkansas, Tennessee, Oklahoma (where it was located adjacent to the Oklahoma City National Memorial), Texas, Louisiana, Mississippi, Alabama, Georgia, and Florida. This traveling exhibit included 9/11 photographs, artifacts, and videos of first-hand accounts. Of critical interest here was the display of steel beams that will be used in the construction of the National September 11 Museum; the visiting public was invited to write on these beams, leaving messages, names, and sentiments that will become a part of the WTC site's built environment.

The Experiential, Visual, and Material Culture of Memory and Tourism

Ethnographic work centered on tourism and tourists at commemorative historical sites engenders a deeper understanding of the powerful experientiality of actual encounters with commemorative landscapes and museum exhibits. It provides empirical evidence for the ways in which prosthetic memories of events and their aftermath are indeed constructed through engagement with the difficult artifacts and experiential displays in museum exhibits, supporting Landsberg's (1997, 2004) arguments for a valuation of experiential modes as legitimate and authentic encounters with historical knowledge, not inauthentic, meaningless, morbid entertainment. Continuing my engagement with a number of my participants beyond the sites under study and encountering, in my everyday routines, those who have been to these and other sites have provided ongoing evidence of the enduring effects of visiting commemorative sites. This combination of both on- and off-site research has rarely been done in one study, and the results of doing this multisited ethnography yielded a significant amount of rich information that otherwise would have remained unknown. In particular, attention to the relationships between on- and off-site cultural practices demonstrated how visiting commemorative sites is indeed part of the social making of these places—sites are continually constructed through ongoing performative narratives of the experience. It is also part of the ongoing making of selves as the identities and subjectivities of tourists are transformed through travel experiences, sometimes in very significant ways.

The various acts of marking place and presence that tourists and locals engage in are a way of making commemorative sites meaningful both individually and collectively. These acts also persist in various visual and material forms far beyond the visit itself, playing a key role in the ongoing creation and articulation of memory and historicity off-site, post-visit. Photography is one of the most central of these acts, a means for making a material and visual record of the experiential moment in order to recollect it in the future and further attribute meanings to the experience and thus the site itself under changing contexts for interpretation. We recollect and (re)experience so very much when we engage with photographs—physical feelings, other things seen, people met, and more. Photos, like souvenirs, evoke narratives and reverie, and even without explicit accompanying oral narration they "tell" others something about what we ourselves saw and inform the subjectivities of those who may never visit the places we photographed. By including a focus on tourist photography I made central the visual (and typically material, even in this digital age) representational practice of tourist photography as a means for interrogating meaning-making and memory via the performativity of sharing photographs with others. Investigation into the actual uses of these photos post-visit revealed the incredibly powerful social and cultural consequences that photographs do indeed still have even in this age of mass visual production and reproduction, both institutional and individual.

Given the contemporary "memory industry" that continues to grow commercially and its relationship to everyday memory practices far beyond the public spaces of historical and commemorative museums and landscapes, a provocative area for additional research lies in further understanding the many ways in which individuals perform the roles of personal historiographers of their own lives. Travel constitutes only one of many subjects of personal historiography, and both the various everyday and extraordinary experiences are represented in similar narrative ways: through photography, the collection of other material culture (such as souvenirs), and the creative assemblages and displays and the sharing of both in everyday spaces (for example, through scrapbooking). Whereas I made an initial foray into this realm in terms of post-travel social practices, future attention to this memory industry may reveal even more about the processes, new and old, through which memory, historicity, and place are constructed, particularly those for a heritage that hurts now and into the future.

Appendix

SELF-ADMINISTERED QUESTIONNAIRE (BASED ON CHALFEN 1987)

(Note: Spaces for open-ended responses have been truncated on this version of the questionnaire.)

This questionnaire must be filled out by an **adult** head of household, female or male. Please indicate who is filling out this questionnaire: _____ female _____ male

Section 1: This section concerns the types of photographic equipment you and members of your household use and/or own. The purpose of this section is to get an idea of what kind of equipment people are using at home and away from home to record activities and events.

1a. Please indicate with a check mark the photographic equipment owned and/or used by members of your household and note the number of such items. Please include any equipment you own but no longer use.

Digital camera _____ Yes _____ No

Total number owned: _____

35-mm camera _____ Yes _____ No

Total number owned: _____

Video recorder _____ Yes _____ No

Total number owned: _____

Polaroid camera   _____ Yes   _____ No
Total number owned: _____
Cellular phone with
photographic imaging   _____ Yes   _____ No
Total number owned: _____
Other: _____   _____ Yes   _____ No
Total number owned: _____

1b. Which of the above do you use the most?

1c. Do you ever use disposable cameras?
_____ Yes   _____ No

1d. If you answered yes on 1c, approximately how many disposable cameras have you used in the last 6 months?
_____ 1–4   _____ 5–8
_____ 9–11   _____ more than 12

1e. Do any of the following reasons apply to your decisions to
use disposable cameras?
Convenience (weight,
cost, etc.)   _____ Yes   _____ No
Forgot regular camera   _____ Yes   _____ No
Do not wish to take expensive
equipment on certain trips   _____ Yes   _____ No
Ease of use (i.e., for kids)   _____ Yes   _____ No
Other (please list): _____

1f. When you have your disposable or 35-mm camera film developed, do you also get a CD of digital images in addition
to the print images?
_____ always   _____ sometimes   _____ never

1g. Which of the following media do you currently produce for
personal use?
_____ Photograph prints
_____ Digital images (JPEGs, etc.)
_____ Slides
_____ Polaroid (instant) prints
_____ Video cassette/digital tape

_____ Video on CD/DVD
_____ other (please list):

1h. Which of the following media makes up your complete photographic collection (i.e., all holdings in your household from the past and in the present)?

_____ Photograph prints
_____ Digital images (JPEGs, etc.)
_____ Slides
_____ Polaroid (instant) prints
_____ Video cassette/digital tape
_____ Video on CD/DVD
_____ 8-mm, 16-mm film reels
_____ other (please list):

1i. If you have a home computer, please mark all of the following that you use it for in regard to photographs:

_____ sending digital photos via email
_____ making webpages for digital photos
_____ editing videos
_____ making scrapbook pages with software
_____ editing digital photos
_____ organizing digital photos with software
_____ scanning photograph prints
_____ other (please list)

Section 2: This section concerns your photographic habits while away from home and specifically while in New York City.

2a. When on vacation or away from home during holidays, do you

_____ *always*
_____ *usually*
_____ *never* take along a camera of some kind?

2b. While on vacation or away from home, who in your immediate household (i.e., self, spouse/partner, child, other) takes the majority of photographs (digital or print)?

2c. While on vacation or away from home, who in your immediate household (i.e., self, spouse/partner, child, other) shoots the most video footage? _____

2d. While on this recent trip to New York City, approximately how many total photographs did you take? _____

2e. While on this recent trip to New York City, approximately how many of these photographs were taken at the WTC (Ground Zero)? _____

2f. Please describe the five most meaningful visual images (print, digital, or video) you took with your own equipment while at the WTC site. You may add comments as to why you consider them important.

2g. Regarding the photos you took, where do you (or plan to) keep or display them? Check all that apply.

_____ communal living space of your home
_____ private living space of your home
_____ place of work
_____ scrapbook
_____ photo album
_____ online webpage/photoshare

2h. Is this your first visit to New York?

_____ Yes _____ No

2i. Which of the following best describes the primary purpose for this recent visit?

business _____ Yes _____ No
vacation _____ Yes _____ No
other _____ Yes
(please list): _____

2j. If this is not your first visit to New York City, have you visited since September 11, 2001 for:

business _____ Yes _____ No
vacation _____ Yes _____ No
other _____ Yes
(please list): _____

Section 3: This section concerns the kinds of souvenirs and other memorabilia items you purchased while on this recent trip to New York City and such items in general. If you did not buy any such items, please go directly to Section 4.

3a. Do you _____ *always* _____ *sometimes* _____ *rarely* _____ *never* purchase items when traveling?

3b. When you purchase souvenirs or memorabilia, who are they for? (Check all that apply)

_____ self   _____ your children

_____ parents   _____ other relatives

_____ close friends   _____ co-workers

_____ neighbors   _____ other (please list):

3c. On this specific trip to New York, whom did you buy items for? (Check all that apply)

_____ self   _____ your children

_____ parents   _____ other relatives

_____ close friends   _____ co-workers

_____ neighbors   _____ other (please list):

3d. Where did you buy items? (Check all that apply)

_____ street vendors   _____ souvenir shops

_____ museums   _____ restaurants

_____ historical sites   _____ other (please list):

3e. On this trip, which of the following items did you purchase? Please provide the number of items purchased and a brief description of each item. (Items listed in table form include: T-shirt, hat, postcard, book, photograph, drawing/ sketch/other artwork, keychain, poster, DVD/CD/VHS, food item.)

3f. If not included in the table above, please list any other items you purchased.

3g. How many of these items are associated with September 11 in some way? _____ If not described in the table above, please provide a description of these items:

3h. What of the following are important to you in selecting souvenirs and memorabilia of places that you have visited?

_____ price   _____ quality
_____ representation of historical importance
_____ representation of the place
_____ representation of a specific experience

3i. Is there any one particular kind of item that you try to collect from every single place you visit (for example, I always collect turtle carvings or artwork, my mother-in-law collects souvenir spoons, and my mother collects postcards of local food items)?

3j. Regarding items that you bought for yourself (besides clothing items), where do you (or plan to) keep or display them? Check all that apply.

_____ communal living space of your home
_____ place of work
_____ photo album
_____ private living space in your home
_____ scrapbook
_____ shadowbox
_____ postcard album/box
_____ other (please list):

Section 4: This section requests basic demographic information. You are not required to provide any information that you do not wish to. To protect your privacy and anonymity, please do not list any specific names, ages, cities, or addresses with the exception of requested information regarding email contact.

4a. What state do you currently reside in? _____

4b. How many members of your household went on this recent trip to New York City? _____

4c. How many reside in your household at this time? _____

4d. Please list the number of members in your household that fall into the age ranges below:

_____ under 1–5	_____ 6–11	_____ 12–18
_____ 19–25	_____ 26–34	_____ 35–40
_____ 41–47	_____ 48–55	_____ 56–60
_____ 61–68	_____ 69–78	_____ over 79

4e. How would you best describe the ethnic composition of you and/or your family?

4f. What is the religious affiliation or affiliations of you and/or your family if any?

4g. What are the occupations of the adults residing in your household (list all that apply, in general terms)?

4h. Do you or anyone else in your household participate in scrapbooking activities?

_____ yes   _____ no

If so, are they

_____ male   _____ female

_____ both males and females

Does anyone attend scrapbooking classes and/or regularly participate in other type of group scrapbooking activities?

_____ yes   _____ no

4i. If in the future I have opportunities to conduct interviews or otherwise continue correspondence, would you be interested in participating?

_____ yes   _____ no

If yes, please provide your <u>first</u> name only or the name you chose for anonymity and your email address:

Notes

Preface

1. Photographer Ian Spiers's detailed account of his harassment may be found at www.brownequalsterrorist.com/.

Chapter 1

1. The 2001 edited volume from Schofield, Johnson, and Beck solely addresses the role of material culture from various 20th century wars as part of "a heritage that hurts." However, in the introductory essay the editors note that the material culture of other acts of violence, atrocity, and tragedy (as they are used in both private and public domains) also forms a part of this heritage.

2. For an on-the-scenes account of the 2001–2002 rescue, recovery, and debris removal process and its many controversies, see William Langewiesche's *American Ground: Unbuilding the World Trade Center* (2003).

3. Arad and Walker's design images and details are at www.wtcsitememorial.org/fin7.html. To view all the submissions, go to www.wtcsitememorial.org/submissions.html and use the search function. Libeskind's "Memorial Foundations" design is at www.daniel-libeskind.com/projects/show-all/memory-foundations/.

4. The original construction of the WTC complex in the 1960s was likewise controversial and disruptive, dislocating small

businesses and destroying residential neighborhoods. Works by Darton (1999); Ganz and Lipton (2003); Ruchelman (1977) provide comprehensive histories of the political, economic, and architectural processes of building the original WTC site.

5. The 20-ton granite block is inscribed: "To honor and remember those who lost their lives on September 11th, 2001, and as a tribute to the enduring spirit of freedom—July Fourth, 2004."

6. The Alliance for Downtown New York (ADNY) is associated with the Lower Manhattan Development Corporation (LMDC).

7. In 2003, 10% of visitors were from Manhattan; 32% were from metro NYC boroughs, suburbs, New York State, and regional mid-Atlantic states; 26% were from other domestic states; and 32% were international visitors (ADNY 2003b:21).

8. Several books and numerous scholarly articles thoroughly critique the production aspect of the WTC site, focusing primarily on the struggles involved in planning the rebuilding effort through a focus on policy, planning, discourse, and civic involvement by victims' family members, survivor groups, schools, and local neighborhood and business organizations. These works generally do not address the ongoing processes of social construction and consumption by a much broader public, both tourists and locals, as they are transpiring. See, for example, Beauregard (2004), Corona (2007), Girard and Stark (2007), Hajer (2005), Kondo (2007), Low (2004), Mollenkopf (2005), Moynihan (2004), and Simpson (2006).

9. See Banks and Morphy (1997), Collier and Collier (1986 [1967]), Hockings (1995), and Pink (2001) for significant discussions of past and present methods and issues in visual anthropology.

10. The questionnaire was based on one used by Chalfen (1987).

11. All participants were asked whether or not they wished to be anonymous in any written results of the research. Thus

the names and other identifying information (such as place of residence and occupation) used in this book may be real or fictitious, depending on the permissions granted by participants.

12. New York Foundation for the Arts Interactive News, NYFA 2006 (www.nyfa.org/level3.asp?id=453&fid=6&sid=17, accessed October 2006).

13. This is the ideology that the living should be remembered in the future, after death, through various kinds of preservationist and creative acts, from the maintenance of cemeteries to the crafting and wearing of mourning jewelry.

Chapter 2

1. The journal *History and Memory: Studies in Representations of the Past* was established in 1991, and since 1990 dozens of special issues in anthropology journals have been dedicated to the topic of memory. *Ethos* presented one of the more recent of these special issues, "The Immanent Past" (Volume 34, Issue 2, March 2006).

2. Among earlier works, the work of Maurice Halbwachs (1992 [1952]) forms the foundational structure for many of these more recent works, particularly his assertion that all memory is socially constructed and performed, and it is highly fragmentary. This assertion contrasts to earlier and primarily psychoanalytic theories that held memory to exist as an entity in the human subconscious or unconscious.

3. Landsberg (2004) and Sturken (1997) both also provide excellent overviews of the history of memory scholarship and significant transformations in social memory-making processes over time and space.

4. Although my approach and conclusions are often at odds with those of MacCannell, I wish to note here that some of his theoretical frameworks (and those in Cohen's later works) have been invaluable to me in to thinking through my research.

5. Given that methodology is tightly linked to the production of theory in ethnographic research, I find this oversight to be disappointing and even damaging, because a lack of methodological transparency may compromise the validity of the theory (Sather-Wagstaff 2008). Among tourism scholars, both Bruner and Harrison make efforts in their work to clearly outline the contours of their fieldsites, how they came to engage with tourists, and some of the methods they used, although Bruner's works would be strengthened by a more explicit discussion of methods.

6. Julia Harrison (2003:39) notes that some exceptions to this include, among a few others, Dann (1996), Desforges (2000), and Gottlieb (1982). There are, of course, more, but this is still an overwhelmingly infrequent practice in tourism studies across disciplines.

7. See G. Gmelch (2004), Marcoux and Legoux (2005), and Sharpley and Stone (2009) for research centered on leading student travel groups and Dekel (2009) on study while working as a tour guide.

8. In terms of absolute origins of work on tourism in anthropology, Nash (1996:1) notes that the first published study was an article by Nuñez (1963).

9. I, too, view travel as a type of modern pilgrimage that is critical to the shaping of one's worldview similar to the ways that religion and religious pilgrimage are for some people. However, what I wish to stress here is the use of a discourse of "primitivism" by scholars such as Graeburn and MacCannell to represent this concept.

10. Crick (1995) also constructively addresses the various ways in which "being in the field" is highly similar to a tourist's holiday away—from issues of communication problems and the simple fact that both are temporary stays to how the ethnographer is often considered a tourist by locals despite arguing otherwise.

Chapter 3

1. According to the ADNY 2003b report, the World Trade Center site was the number-one tourist destination in Lower Manhattan during 2003, followed by the South Street Seaport (for 46% of domestic and 47% of international tourists) and the Statue of Liberty/Ellis Island (for 53% of domestic and 64% of international tourists).

2. In the mainstream media the terms *necrotourism, terror tourism, death tourism/tourist*, and *disaster tourism/tourist* are also common. The last term is used frequently in news articles reporting on post-disaster tourism and humanitarian aid travel to affected areas following the massive 2004 Indian Ocean tsunami, Hurricane Katrina in 2005, and the Haiti earthquake in 2010.

3. Sharpley and Stone (2009) and Stone (2006) have pursued creating a typology of dark tourism that works to ameliorate this flattening through a darkest (history and education-centric) to lightest (commercial and entertainment-centric).

4. The special issue (Winter 1996, Vol. 12:1) is titled *Dark Tourism: A Conceptual Approach to Tourism* and contains four articles, including one authored by Lennon and Foley that outlines the development of the John F. Kennedy Sixth Floor Museum at Dealey Plaza.

5. Tourists often expressed frustration at not knowing what to expect at the WTC site, and they attributed their lack of knowledge on what they perceived to be highly limited media coverage of the aftermath and the current rebuilding process. When asked what news sources they rely on, responses overwhelmingly privileged local television and newspaper media. Those who did use the internet for email, shopping, and non-local news tended to use online news feed resources such as Yahoo news (http://news.yahoo.com) and other generalized news feeds often directly linked with internet access service accounts.

6. One extreme example of this position would be to claim that only direct relatives of those who died during the Holocaust should be allowed visit Holocaust sites. This renders such sites as graveyards inaccessible except for a closed, controlled population rather than accessible for all, to widely disseminate knowledge that aims, however optimistically, to prevent such acts of atrocity in the future.

7. As a fundamental part of my conceptualization of memory-making, I find the distinction that scholars make between the "experiential" and "cognitive" to be a problem, because it artificially separates the "mind" from the "body" of the learning, knowing, and performing subject.

8. www.humorisdead.com/groundzero (accessed March 2002).

9. Various groups wish for "The Cross" to be included in the formal memorial landscape, but others strongly oppose this.

10. www.nyopinion.com (accessed May 2003).

11. In contrast, professional and journalistic photography is considered serious, acceptable, and necessary, and it has been highly celebrated in numerous exhibits and publications. In 2006 Joel Meyerowitz, perhaps the most celebrated of photographers who produced images of 9/11 and the aftermath, published *Aftermath: The World Trade Center Archive,* and photographs from this collection are being exhibited around the world. However, photojournalists exhibited some of the most unethical and crass photographic behaviors I observed at the WTC site. For example, on the 2006 anniversary, I witnessed two photographers wearing media tags shooting photos of a woman crouched down against the viewing wall, holding her knees and crying. They shot dozens of photos and then walked away without ever approaching the woman to ask her name, find out if she was okay, ask permission to take or use her photo, or find out anything about her story.

Chapter 4

1. http://groundzerothemepark.com, accessed July 2003; (N.B.: Although I did see pins, postcards, booklets, and flags sold

at the WTC site [along with crystal paperweights, toy fire trucks, key chains, lanyards, and photographs], I never once personally saw any of the gold-plated "Cross" reproductions that this writer mentions.)

2. Even the cornerstone for the Freedom Tower is not immune to such critiques of consumption versus commemoration. Journalist David Dunlap argues that the cornerstone's design, from the materials to the typeface used, "reflect the inherent ambiguity of the project: a solemn memorial to 2,749 lives lost in the worst single catastrophe in New York history that is simultaneously supposed to be a defiant restatement of the city's commercial gigantism" (2004).

3. Unlicensed peripatetic vendors (typically carrying only one type of item such as flags, photographs, or booklets) would generally not speak to me or anyone else at great length. They are actively violating the signs prohibiting sales on the site proper; thus if anyone was to complain about them to the police, they would be forcibly removed—I witnessed this on several occasions. These vendors thus avoided conversation beyond that necessary for selling an item. In addition, they tended to be the most assertive and rude of all vendors. They were seen rushing to tour bus doors as they opened and approaching tourists as they made their way up the stairs from the transit station before anyone even had a chance to set foot on the WTC site sidewalk.

4. Gottdiener also claims that work no longer defines self or is "the key existential experience behind lifestyle choices" and that consumption, in its various forms, is the dominant way that everyday life is experienced (2000:ix). As a result of my research, I challenge this claim: when we introduced ourselves, tourists privileged where they were from and what they did for a living over other aspects of their identities. Their introductions indicate that one's occupation is still very much a central modality for expressing self to others and for framing everyday, past, and future experiences and desires.

5. Information on these sites can be found at www.time-elevator-jerusalem.co.il and www.nazarethvillage.com/.

6. It is primarily in the eyes of scholars who study these sites that they appear so geographically omnipresent. To the general public, who engages with certain historical sites primarily when traveling versus through scholarly research, these sites are considered special, unique, and rare, not "just around every corner." Only a few tourists in my study had visited more than one Holocaust museum or site.

7. The arguments about over-consumption and how to remedy it frequently center on transforming modes of consumption from those that support the gross inequalities of the capitalist world-market system to those that are more socially responsible, supporting a more equitable distribution of monetary resources and being less destructive to the physical environment. Kimberly Lau makes a cogent argument in *New Age Capitalism: Making Money East of Eden* (2000) for how even the most socially conscientious consumption has a literal and symbolic high price. According to Lau, "buying green" or organic and supporting local or other sustainability-centered businesses often require higher levels of spending (owing to the higher costs of the goods and services produced) and thus, paradoxically, buyers who have a higher income are thus able to be "socially responsible consumers."

8. Such a position assumes that there are ontological, inherent, and stable meanings for things and activities. However, linguistics provides evidence for the fundamental arbitrariness of meaning, and so, if informed by this, one would view all sign values of all things and activities as arbitrary and subject to constant manipulation rather than as traceable to one "real" and thus authentic meaning. Similarly, Bruner finds the fundamental issue of the "authentic" to be a "red herring" in that all cultural articulations can be understood as authentic because of their performativity—each iteration, no matter how different, is an authentic cultural performance (2005:5).

Chapter 5

1. See www.wingtv.net/ for more information on this group.
2. ArtAID (www.artaid.org/) has produced a number of commemorative posters for 9/11 as well as other tragedies, such as Hurricane Katrina, various major fires, murders of police officers, and the Virginia Tech shootings. According to their website, "ArtAID contributes to community by providing artists with meaningful opportunities to serve humanitarian causes, supports artistic practices in creating works and developing projects that foster healing and inspiration in times of need. ArtAID operates a 1st Response capability to respond to unforeseen crisis events, loss of life, and tragedy."
3. In some cases, such as that of the Pentagon after September 11, 2001, and the Lockerbie, Scotland, air disaster, proximity to the site is heavily restricted for security and investigation reasons, and thus the assemblages absolutely must be located elsewhere.
4. Now found throughout the world, these new roadside cross assemblages have evolved from far older cultural practices of marking the sites of unexpected death, specifically the construction and emplacement of *descansos* ("resting places"—used to describe roadside markers for a place of death) in the landscapes of the U.S. Southwest and parts of Latin America.
5. Items left at the Vietnam Veterans Memorial in Washington, D.C., have been collected since 1984, and numerous items are on permanent display in the Smithsonian National Museum of American History. In 2007 the number of items from the Memorial that are housed in the archive surpassed 100,000.
6. For information on the 9/11 Memorial Preview Site, construction updates, and a Google Earth map of the WTC site plans, see: www.national911memorial.org/site/Page Server?pagename=New_Visit_Page.

Chapter 6

1. The WTC Tribute Center (www.tributewtc.org/index.php) opened in September 2006 at 120 Liberty Street on the southeast edge of the WTC site.

2. In contrast, the materials and designs for Holocaust memorials tend to be endowed by their designers with very different meanings. In Berlin, the field of unmarked, uneven pillars and pathways in Peter Eisenman's Monument to the Murdered Jews of Europe are intended to represent uncertainty, their placement constructed so that only a few people can walk between them at a time, evoking a feeling of isolation, imbalance, and unease. Unlike the living landscapes of contemporary U.S. memorials (including those built and yet to be built for 9/11), there is no comfort to be found in Eisenman's stark field of concrete.

3. This is of particular interest given that, in brochures and on signage, the memorial landscape in Oklahoma City is called "The Symbolic Memorial."

4. Anti-Muslim outrage continues in 2010 as plans to open an Islamic center and mosque within blocks of the WTC have been announced.

5. President Clinton opened his comments during the dedication of the Memorial with: "We are here on sacred ground." An independently published book of photographs is titled *Angels over Oklahoma City,* and the media used similar religious/spiritual discourse in articles covering the event and the building of the Memorial.

6. In contrast, the "Here Is New York: Remembering 9/11" photographic exhibit in Manhattan and Chicago included an image of bodies falling from the WTC towers and a photograph of the body of Father Mychal being carried from the WTC rubble by rescue workers.

7. As of September 2006 this artifact has been on display in the Tribute Center. The Center has on display a number of objects that are slated for inclusion in the National September 11 Memorial.

8. Research on the impact of the computer-based system in terms of changes in the content and format of markings at the Oklahoma City Memorial is now part of a current project on the use of technology in memorial museums both for exhibits and for participatory commemorative activities.
9. The 911 Digital Archive: http://911digitalarchive.org/. To browse the collection go to http://911digitalarchive.org/galleries.php?collection_id=31.

Chapter 7

1. For work that includes discussions of the lived, social, and performative aspects of tourists' photography from an ethnographic and tourist-centered perspective, see Bruner (2005), Harrison (2003), and Edensor (1998). Richard Chalfen's book (1987) also provides a more comprehensive ethnographic treatment of vernacular photography in the late-20th-century, analog camera era.
2. The questionnaire was based on one used by Chalfen (1987).
3. The response rate was unusually high (61%) for a self-administered, unmonitored questionnaire. As with my on-site conversations, I attribute some of the success with the questionnaire to the eagerness that tourists had for sharing their experiences with me, both those of September 11, 2001 and those of visiting the site.
4. This was not entirely unexpected, given that over a quarter of U.S. households engage in scrapbooking and that participants are typically women from the middle-class economic status that enables moderate travel to a city such as New York as well as the expenditures needed for this hobby. Since its beginnings in the mid-1990s, the scrapbooking industry has grown to 2.5 billion dollars annually, and the costs of this hobby, although reasonable, do require outputs of both money and leisure time (see Creating Keepsakes 2004). One of my future ethnographic projects will focus exclusively on contemporary scrapbooking practices as a significant part of the growing nostalgia and memory industry.

5. Daniel also collected very valuable, rare antique coins, but these were kept in his home office, a space used by no one but himself.

Chapter 8

1. The 9/11 Truth Movement website is at www.911truth.org/.
2. Owing to security issues, the United States Holocaust Memorial Museum does not have any space for commemorative assemblages. However, an exception was made to this precaution following the death of museum security officer Tyrone Johns on June 10, 2009. While I was doing research there, white supremacist and antisemite James von Brun shot and killed Officer Johns while he was on duty at the front entrance to the Museum. I immediately made it clear that the museum needed to find a way to allow a public commemorative assemblage despite the security rules. They did, by establishing an area outside the guardhouse. Both tourists and locals came to the museum over the next week and contributed items to the commemorative assemblage for Officer Johns.

References

Albers, Patricia, and William James. 1988. Travel Photography: A Methodological Approach. *Annals of Tourism Research* 15:134–58.

Alliance for Downtown New York (ADNY). 2003a. *The Downtown Report—Winter 2003.* New York: ADNY.

———. 2003b. *State of Lower Manhattan.* New York: ADNY.

———. 2008. *Lower Manhattan Hotel Guest Study.* New York: Audience Research & Analysis for ADNY.

Altebrando, Julie. 2001. Ground Zero: Heartfelt homage or tacky tourist trap? *All Info about New York City Online Newsletter*, electronic document, http://nyc.allinfoabout.com/features/groundzero.html, accessed February 2, 2002.

Amit, Vered. 2000. Introduction: Constructing the Field. In *Constructing the Field: Ethnographic Fieldwork in the Contemporary World.* Vered Amit, ed., pp. 1–18. London: Routledge.

Anderson, Benedict. 1991. *Imagined Communities: Reflections on the Origin and Spread of Nationalism.* London: Verso.

Appadurai, Arjun. 1986. Introduction: Commodities and the Politics of Value. In *The Social Life of Things: Commodities in Cultural Perspective.* Arjun Appadurai, ed., pp. 3–63. Cambridge: Cambridge University Press.

Archibold, Randal. 2003. Living at Ground Zero and Tiring of the Neighborhood Sideshow. *The New York Times,* September 9. Electronic document, www.nytimes.com, accessed September 21, 2003.

Aramberri, Julio. 2003. Review: Julia Harrison's Being a Tourist: Finding Meaning in Pleasure Travel. *Annals of Tourism Research* 30(4):964–66.

Austin, John L. 1975 [1962]. *How to Do Things with Words.* Cambridge: Harvard University Press.

Bakewell, Liza. 1998. Image Acts. *American Anthropologist* 100(1):22–32.

Banks, Marcus, and Howard Morphy, eds. 1997. *Rethinking Visual Anthropology.* New Haven, CT: Yale University Press.

Barthes, Roland. 1981. *Camera Lucida: Reflections on Photography.* Richard Howard, trans. New York: Hill and Wang.

Bauman, Zygmunt. 1996. From Pilgrim to Tourist: A Short History of Identity. In *Questions of Cultural Identity.* Stuart Hall and Paul du Gay, eds., pp. 18–36. London: Sage.

Beauregard, Robert. 2004. Mistakes Were Made: Rebuilding the World Trade Center, Phase 1. *International Planning Studies* 9(2-3): 139–53.

Beech, John. 2000. The Enigma of Holocaust Sites as Tourist Attractions—the Case of Buchenwald. *Managing Leisure* 5(1):29–41.

Benjamin, Walter. 1968. *Illuminations.* Hannah Arendt, ed. Harry Zohn, trans. New York: Schocken Books.

Bischoff, Howard. 2002. Local Tourist Offers Impressions of New York City and WTC Site. *Los Altos Town Crier,* September 11, electronic document, http://latc.com/2002/09/11/news/coversto2.html, accessed September 30, 2002.

Blom, Thomas. 2000. Morbid Tourism: A Postmodern Niche with an Example from Althorp. *Norwegian Journal of Geography* 54:29–36.

Bodnar, John. 1992. *Remaking America: Public Memory, Commemoration, and Patriotism in the Twentieth Century.* Princeton, NJ: Princeton University Press.

Boorstin, Daniel. 1961. *The Image: A Guide to Pseudo-events in America.* New York: Harper and Row.

Bouquet, Mary. 2000. The Family Photographic Condition. *Visual Anthropology Review* 16(1):2–19.

Bourdieu, Pierre. 1990 [1965]. *Photography: A Middle-brow Art.* Stanford, CA: Stanford University Press.

Broderick, Mick, and Mark Gibson. 2005. Mourning, Monomyth, and Memorabilia. In *The Selling of 9/11: How a National Tragedy Became a Commodity.* Dana Heller, ed., pp. 200–20. New York: Palgrave.

224

Bruner, Edward M. 1984. Introduction: The Opening Up of Anthropology. In *Text, Play, and Story: The Construction and Reconstruction of Self and Society*. Edward M. Bruner, ed. 1983 Proceedings of the American Ethnological Society, pp. 1–16. Washington, D.C.: American Anthropological Association.

———. 1989. Cannibals, Tourists, and Ethnographers. *Cultural Anthropology* 4:438–45.

———. 1993. Lincoln's New Salem as a Contested Site. *Museum Anthropology* 17(3):14–25.

———. 1994. Abraham Lincoln as Authentic Reproduction: A Critique of Postmodernism. *American Anthropologist* 96:397–415.

———. 1995. The Ethnographer/Tourist in Indonesia. In *International Tourism: Identity and Change*. Marie-Françoise Lanfant, John Allcock, and Edward M. Bruner, eds., pp. 224–41. London: Sage.

———. 2005. *Culture on Tour: Ethnographies of Travel*. Chicago: University of Chicago Press.

Butler, David. 2001. Whitewashing Plantations: The Commodification of a Slave-Free Antebellum South. In *Slavery, Contested Heritage, and Thanatourism*, Graham Dann and A.V. Seaton, eds., pp. 163–75. New York: Haworth Press.

Butler, Judith. 1990. Performative Acts and Gender Constitution: An Essay in Phenomenology and Feminist Theory. In *Performing Feminisms: Feminist Critical Theory and Theatre*, pp. 270–82, Sue-Ellen Case, ed. Baltimore: Johns Hopkins University Press.

Chalfen, Richard. 1987. *Snapshot Versions of Life*. Bowling Green, OH: Bowling Green State University Press.

Chidester, David, and Edward Linenthal. 1995. Introduction. In *American Sacred Space*. David Chidester and Edward Linenthal, eds., pp. 1–42. Bloomington: Indiana University Press.

Civic Alliance. 2005. *Summary Proceedings of the World Trade Center Memorial Museum Programming Workshop*. New York: Civic Alliance to Rebuild Downtown New York.

Clark Hine, Darlene. 1994. *Hindsight: Black Women and the Re-Construction of American History*. New York: Carlson Publishing.

Clarke, John. 2004. What's It For? The Work of Anthropology and the Work of 9/11. *Critique of Anthropology* 24(1):9–14.

Cohen, Erik. 1974. Who Is a Tourist? A Conceptual Clarification. *Sociological Review* 22:527–55.

———. 1988. Authenticity and Commoditization in Tourism. *Annals of Tourism Research* 15:371–86.

Cole, Tim. 1999. *Selling the Holocaust: From Auschwitz to Schindler. How History Is Bought, Packaged, and Sold.* New York: Routledge.

Coleman, Simon, and Mike Crang. 2002. Grounded Tourists, Travelling Theory. In *Tourism: Between Place and Performance.* Simon Coleman and Mike Crang, eds., pp. 1–17. New York: Berghahn.

Collier, John, and Malcolm Collier. 1986 [1967]. *Visual Anthropology: Photography as a Research Method.* Albuquerque: University of New Mexico Press.

Comaroff, Jean, and John L. Comaroff. 2000. Millennial Capitalism: First Thoughts on a Second Coming. *Public Culture* 12(2):291–343.

Corona, Victor. 2007. Voices and Visions of Lower Manhattan: Organizing Civic Expression in Post-9/11 Public Hearings. *Journal of Civil Society* 3(2):119–35.

Crang, Mike. 1997. Picturing Practices: Research Through the Tourist Gaze. *Progress in Human Geography* 21(3):289–305.

Crapanzano, Greg. 2007. Failing to Respect the Victims of 9-11: Plans for Ground Zero Memorial Disrespect Memory of the Victims. *The Cavalier Daily*, April 27 (www.cavalierdaily.com/CVArticle.asp?ID=30354&pid=1588, accessed April 2007).

Crawshaw, Carol, and John Urry. 1997. Tourism and the Photographic Eye. In *Touring Cultures: Transformations of Travel and Theory.* Chris Rojek and John Urry, eds., pp. 176–95. London: Routledge.

Creating Keepsakes. 2004. *Report: National Survey of Scrapbooking in America.* Provo, UT: Creating Keepsakes, Inc.

Crick, Malcolm. 1995. The Anthropologist as Tourist: An Identity in Question. In *International Tourism: Identity and Change.* Marie-Françoise Lanfant, John Allcock, and Edward M. Bruner, eds., pp. 205–23. London: Sage.

Csikszentmihalyi, Mihaly, and Eugene Rochberg-Halton. 1981. *The Meaning of Things: Domestic Symbols and the Self.* Cambridge: Cambridge University Press.

Dann, Graham. 1996. Tourists' Images of a Destination: An Alternative Analysis. *Journal of Tourism and Marketing* 5(1-2):41–55.

Dann, Graham, and Robert Potter. 2001. Supplanting the Planters: Hawking Heritage in Barbados. In *Slavery, Contested Heritage, and Thanatourism.* Dann Graham and A.V. Seaton, eds., pp. 51–84. New York: Haworth Press.

Dann, Graham, and A.V. Seaton. 2001. Introduction. In *Slavery, Contested Heritage, and Thanatourism.* Graham Dann and A.V. Seaton, eds., pp. 1–29. New York: Haworth Press.

Darton, Eric. 1999. *Divided We Stand: A Biography of New York's World Trade Center.* New York: Basic Books.

de Certeau, Michel. 1984. *The Practice of Everyday Life.* Berkeley and Los Angeles: University of California Press.

Dekel, Irit. 2009. Ways of Looking: Observation and Transformation at the Holocaust Memorial, Berlin. *Memory Studies* 2(1):71–86.

Denzin, Norman, and Yvonna Lincoln. 2003. Introduction: 9/11 in American Culture. In *9/11 in American Culture.* Norman Denzin and Yvonna Lincoln, eds., pp. xiii–vii. Walnut Creek, CA: AltaMira Press.

Desforges, Luke. 2000. Traveling the World: Identity and Travel Biography. *Annals of Tourism Research* 27(4):926–45.

Dissanayake, Ellen. 1990. *What Is Art For?* Seattle: University of Washington Press.

Douglas, Mary, and Baron Isherwood. 1996 [1979]. *The World of Goods: Toward an Anthropology of Consumption.* New York: Routledge.

Duffy, Terrence. 2004. Museums of "Human Suffering" and the Struggle for Human Rights. In *Museum Studies: An Anthology of Contexts.* Bettina Messias Carbonell, ed., pp. 117–22. Oxford: Blackwell.

Dunlap, David. 2004. A 9/11 Cornerstone, Chiseled with a New York Accent, *The New York Times*, July 8. Electronic document, http://nytimes.com, accessed July 10, 2004.

Edensor, Tim. 1998. *Tourists at the Taj: Performance and Meaning at a Symbolic Site.* London: Routledge.

———. 2002. *National Identity, Popular Culture and Everyday Life.* New York: Berg.

Edwards, Elizabeth. 1997. Beyond the Boundary: A Consideration of the Expressive in Photography and Anthropology. In *Rethinking Visual Anthropology.* Marcus Banks and Howard Morphy, eds., pp. 53–80. New Haven, CT: Yale University Press.

Edwards, Elizabeth. 1999. Photographs as Objects of Memory. In *Material Memories: Design and Evocation*. Marius Kwint, Christopher Breward, and Jeremy Aynsley, eds., pp. 221–36. Oxford: Berg.

———. 2006. Photographs and the Sound of History. *Visual Anthropology Review* 21(1/2): 27–46.

Elsaesser, Thomas. 1996. Subject Positions, Speaking Positions: From Holocaust, Our Hitler, and Heimat to Shoah and Schindler's List. In *The Persistence of History: Cinema, Television, and the Modern Event*. Vivian Sobchack, ed., pp. 145–83. New York: Routledge.

Erikson, Kai. 2005. Epilogue: The Geography of Disaster. In *Wounded City: The Social Impact of 9/11*. Nancy Foner, ed., pp. 351–62. New York: Russell Sage Foundation.

Eskew, Glenn. 2001. From Civil War to Civil Rights: Selling Alabama as Heritage Tourism. In *Slavery, Contested Heritage, and Thanatourism*, Graham Dann and A.V. Seaton, eds., pp. 201–14. New York: Haworth Press.

Fight Club. 1999. David Fincher, dir. 139 min. Fox 2000 Pictures. Century City.

Foote, Kenneth. 2001 [1997]. *Shadowed Ground: America's Landscapes of Violence and Tragedy*. Austin: University of Texas Press.

Foucault, Michel. 1980. *Power/Knowledge: Selected Interviews and Other Writings 1972–77,* Colin Gordon, ed., Colin Gordon, Leo Marshall, John Mepham, and Kate Soper, trans. New York: Pantheon.

Franklin, Adrian. 2003. *Tourism: An Introduction.* London: Sage.

Ganz, James, and Eric Lipton. 2003. *City in the Sky.* New York: Times Books.

Geertz, Clifford. 1996. Cultural Diplomacy. Keynote address, Tourism and Heritage Management confererence. Yogyakarta, Indonesia, October 1996.

Gell, Alfred. 1998. *Art and Agency: An Anthropological Theory.* Oxford: Oxford University Press.

Gillis, John, ed. 1994. *Commemorations: The Politics of National Identity.* Princeton, NJ: Princeton University Press.

Girard, Monique, and David Stark. 2007. Socio-Technologies of Assembly: Sense Making and Demonstration in Rebuilding Lower Manhattan. In *Governance and Information Technology: From Electronic Government to Information Government*. Viktor

Mayer-Schönberger and David Lazar, eds., pp. 145–76. Cambridge, MA: MIT Press.

Glanz, James. 2003. *City in the Sky: The Rise and Fall of the World Trade Center.* New York: Times Books.

Glassberg, David. 2001. *Sense of History: The Place of the Past in American History.* Amherst: University of Massachusetts Press.

Gmelch, George. 2004. Let's Go Europe: What Student Tourists Really Learn. In *Tourists and Tourism*, Sharon Gmelch, ed., pp. 419–32. Long Grove, IL: Waveland Press.

Gmelch, Sharon. 2004. Why Tourism Matters. In *Tourists and Tourism*, Sharon Gmelch, ed., pp. 2–21. Long Grove, IL: Waveland Press.

Gottdeiner, Mark. 1997. *The Theming of America: Dreams, Visions, and Commercial Spaces.* New York: Westview Press.

———. 2000. The Consumption of Space and Spaces of Consumption. In *New Forms of Consumption: Consumers, Culture, and Commodification*, Mark Gottdiener, ed., pp. 265–85. Lanham, MD: Rowman & Littlefield.

Gottlieb, Alma. 1982. Americans' Vacations. *Annals of Tourism Research* 9(2):165–88.

Graeburn, Nelson. 1977. Tourism: The Sacred Journey. In *Hosts and Guests: The Anthropology of Tourism.* Valene Smith, ed. pp. 21–37. Philadelphia: University of Pennsylvania Press.

———. 2004. Secular Ritual: A General Theory of Tourism. In *Tourists and Tourism*, Sharon Gmelch, ed., pp. 23–34. Long Grove, IL: Waveland Press.

Greenspan, Elizabeth. 2006. *Scaling Tragedy: Memorialization and Globalization at the World Trade Center Site.* Ph.D. dissertation, University of Pennsylvania.

Grider, Sylvia. 2001. Spontaneous Shrines: A Modern Response to Tragedy and Disaster. *New Directions in Folklore* 5. Electronic document, www.temple.edu/isllc/newfolk/shrines.html, accessed January 15, 2009.

Gutman, Yifat. 2009. Where Do We Go From Here: The Pasts, Presents and Futures of Ground Zero. *Memory Studies* 2(1):55–70.

Hajer, Maarten. 2005. Rebuilding Ground Zero: The Politics of Performance. *Planning Theory & Practice* 6(4):445–64.

Haldrup, Michael, and Jonas Larsen. 2003. The Family Gaze. *Tourist Studies* 3:23–46.

Hall, Stuart. 1990. Cultural Identity and Diaspora. In *Identity: Community, Culture, Difference.* Jonathan Rutherford, ed., pp. 222–37. New York: Lawrence & Wishart.

Hammond, Joyce. 2001. Photography, Tourism, and the Kodak Hula Show. *Visual Anthropology* 14(1):1–32.

Handler, Richard, and Eric Gable. 1997. *The New History in an Old Museum: Creating the Past at Colonial Williamsburg.* Durham, NC: Duke University Press.

Harrison, Julia. 2003. *Being A Tourist: Finding Meaning in Pleasure Tourism.* Vancouver: University of British Columbia Press.

Haskins, Ekaterina, and Justin DeRose. 2003. Memory, Visibility, and Public Space: Reflections on Commemoration(s) of 9/11. *Space and Culture* 6:377–93.

Hastrup, Kirsten and Karen Fog Olwig. 1997. Introduction. In *Siting Culture: The Shifting Anthropological Object,* Karen Fog Olwig and Kirsten Hastrup, eds., pp. 1–14. New York: Routledge.

Hill, John. 2006. To Remember or to Forget? *New York Foundation for the Arts Interactive News*, Electronic document, www.nyfa.org/level3.asp?id=453&fid=6&sid=17, accessed May 27, 2006.

Hirsch, Marianne. 1997. *Family Frames: Photography, Narrative, and Postmemory.* Cambridge: Harvard University Press.

Hockings, Paul, ed. 1995. *Principles of Visual Anthropology.* Berlin: Mouton de Gruyter.

Hoffer, Jan. 2002. 9-11 Profiteering at WTC Site Called Immoral, Illegal. WABC News. February 26.

Holguín, Sandie. 2005. National Spain Invites You: Battlefield Tourism during the Spanish Civil War. *American Historical Review* 110(5):1399–426.

Hooper-Greenhill, Eilean. 2000. *Museums and the Interpretation of Visual Culture.* London: Routledge.

Hughes, Rachel. 2008. Dutiful Tourism: Encountering the Cambodian Genocide. *Asia Pacific Viewpoint* 49(3):318–30.

Hummon, David. 1988. Tourist Worlds: Tourist Advertising, Ritual, and American Culture. *Sociological Quarterly* 29(2):179–202.

Hurley, Molly, and James Trimarco. 2004. Morality and Merchandise: Vendors, Visitors, and Police at New York City's Ground Zero. *Critique of Anthropology* 24(1):51–78.

Huyssen, Andreas. 2003. *Present Pasts: Urban Palimpsests and the Politics of Memory.* Stanford, CA: Stanford University Press.

Jakle, John. 1985. *The Tourist: Travel in Twentieth-century North America.* Lincoln: University of Nebraska Press.

Kirshenblatt-Gimblett, Barbara. 1998. *Destination Culture: Tourism, Museums, and Heritage.* Berkeley and Los Angeles: University of California Press.

Kondo, Tamiyo. 2007. Rebuilding Planning after WTC 9.11 Attack in Lower Manhattan: Towards Collaborative Planning by Stakeholder Participation. Paper presented, 2nd International Conference on Urban Disaster Reduction. Taipei, Taiwan. November 2007.

Küchler, Sharon. 1993. Landscape as Memory: The Mapping of Process and its Representation in Melanesian Society. In *Landscape, Politics, and Perspectives.* Barbara Bender, ed., pp. 85–106. Providence: Berg.

Kugelmass, Jack. 1994. Why We Go to Poland: Holocaust Tourism as Secular Ritual. In *The Art of Memory: Holocaust Memorials in History.* James Young, ed., pp. 174–84. Munich: Prestel-Verlag.

Landsberg, Alison. 1997. America, the Holocaust, and the Mass Culture of Memory: Toward a Radical Politics of Empathy. *New German Critique* 71:63–86.

————. 2004. *Prosthetic Memory: The Transformation of American Remembrance in the Age of Mass Culture.* New York: Columbia University Press.

Langewiesche, William. 2003. *American Ground: Unbuilding the World Trade Center.* New York: North Point Press/Farrar, Straus, and Giroux.

Larsen, Jonas. 2005. Families Seen Sightseeing: Performativity of Tourist Photography. *Space and Culture* 8(4): 416–34.

Lau, Kimberly. 2000. *New Age Capitalism: Making Money East of Eden.* Philadelphia: University of Pennsylvania Press.

Lefebvre, Henri. 1991 [1974]. *The Production of Space,* Donald Nicholson-Smith, trans. Cambridge: Blackwell.

Lehon, Dara. 2003. Fighting "Ground Zero" as a Phrase and a Tourist Trap. *Downtown Express.* Electronic document, www.downtownexpress.com/de_21/talkingpoint.html, accessed November 6, 2003.

Lennon, John, and Malcolm Foley. 2000. *Dark Tourism: The Attraction of Death and Disaster.* London: Continuum.

Leslie, Esther. 1999. Souvenirs and Forgetting: Walter Benjamin's Memory-work. In *Material Memories: Design and Evocation.* Marius Kwint, Christopher Breward, and Jeremy Aynsley, eds., pp. 107–22. Oxford: Berg.

Linenthal, Edward. 1995. *Preserving Memory: The Struggle to Create America's Holocaust Museum.* New York: Penguin.

————. 2001. *The Unfinished Bombing: Oklahoma City in American Memory.* New York: Oxford.

Lisle, Debbie. 2004. Gazing at Ground Zero: Tourism, Voyeurism and Spectacle. *Journal for Cultural Research* 5(1):3–21.

Low, Setha M. 2000. *On the Plaza: The Politics of Public Space and Culture.* Austin: University of Texas Press.

————. 2002. Lessons from Imagining the World Trade Center Site: An Examination of Public Space and Culture. *Anthropology & Education Quarterly* 33(3):395–405.

Low, Setha M. 2004. The Memorialization of September 11: Dominant and Local Discourses on the Rebuilding of the World Trade Center Site. *American Ethnologist* 31(3):326–39.

Lowenthal, David. 2005 [1985]. *The Past Is a Foreign Country.* Cambridge: Cambridge University Press.

Lury, Celia. 1998. *Prosthetic Culture: Photography, Memory and Identity.* New York: Routledge.

MacCannell, Dean. 1999 [1976]. *The Tourist: A New Theory of the Leisure Class.* Berkeley and Los Angeles: University of California Press.

Manning, Kay. 2001. A Process of Healing. *Chicago Tribune,* December 10.

Marcoux , Jean Sébastien, and Renaud Legoux. 2005. Ground Zero: A Contested Market. *Consumption, Markets and Culture* 8(3):241–59.

Miller, Daniel. 1993. A Theory of Christmas. In *Unwrapping Christmas,* Daniel Miller, ed., pp. 3–37. Oxford: Oxford University Press.

————. 1997. *Capitalism: An Ethnographic Approach.* New York: Berg.

————. 2005. Materiality: An Introduction. In *Materiality,* Daniel Miller, ed., pp. 1–50. Durham, NC: Duke University Press.

Mintz, Lawrence. 2004. In a Sense Abroad: Theme Parks and Simulated Tourism. In *Tourists and Tourism*, Sharon Gmelch, ed., pp. 183–92. Long Grove, IL: Waveland Press.

Mollenkopf, David. 2005. Contentious City: The Politics of Recovery in New York City. New York: Russell Sage Foundation.

Morgan, Nigel, and Annette Pritchard. 2005. On Souvenirs and Metonymy: Narratives of Memory, Metaphor, and Materiality. *Tourist Studies* 5(1):29–53.

Moynihan, Donald. 2004. Public Participation after 9/11: Rethinking and Rebuilding Lower Manhattan. *Group Facilitation* 6:117–26.

Murdock, Graham, and Sarah Pink. 2005. Picturing Practices: Visual Anthropology and Media Ethnography. In *Media Anthropology*. Eric Rothenbuhler and Mihai Coman, eds., pp. 149–61. Thousand Oaks, CA: Sage.

Muzaini, Hamzah, Peggy Teo, and Brenda Yeoh. 2007. Intimations of Postmodernity in Dark Tourism: The Fate of Hisotry at Fort Siloso, Singapore. *Journal of Tourism and Culture Change* 5(1):28–45.

Nash, Dennison. 1996. *Anthropology of Tourism*. Oxford: Pergamon.

———. 2001. On Travelers, Ethnographers, and Tourists. *Annals of Tourism Research* 28(2):493–96.

Ness, Sally Ann. 2005. Tourism-terrorism: The Landscaping of Consumption and the Darker Side of Place. *American Ethnologist* 32(1):118–40.

Neumann, Mark. 1988. Wandering through the Museum: Experience and Identity in a Spectator Culture. *Border/Lines* 12:19–27.

Nora, Pierre. 1989. Between Memory and History: Les Lieux de Mémoire. *Representations* 26:7–25.

Nuñez, Theron. 1963. Tourism, Tradition, and Acculturation: Weekendismo in a Mexican Village. *Ethnology* 2(3):347–52.

Ohnuki-Tierney, Emiko. 1990. Introduction: The Historicization of Anthropology. In *Culture through Time: Anthropological Approaches*. Emiko Ohnuki-Tierney, ed., pp. 1–25. Stanford, CA: Stanford University Press.

Osborne, Peter. 2000. *Travelling Light: Photography, Travel, and Visual Culture*. Manchester: Manchester University Press.

Peirce, Charles S. 1940. Logic as Semiotic: The Theory of Signs. In *The Philosophy of C. S. Peirce: Selected Writings*. Justus Bucher, ed., pp. 98–104. London: Routledge.

Pink, Sarah. 2001. *Doing Visual Anthropology: Images, Media, and Representation in Research.* London: Sage.

Relph, Edward. 1976. *Place and Placelessness.* London: Pion.

Rojek, Chris. 1993. *Ways of Escape: Modern Transformations in Leisure and Travel.* Lanham, MD: Rowman & Littlefield.

———. 1997. Indexing, Dragging, and the Social Construction of Tourist Sights. In *Touring Cultures: Transformations of Travel and Theory.* Chris Rojek and John Urry, eds., pp. 52–74. London: Routledge.

Rosenthal, John. 2004. The Future of Ground Zero: Daniel Libeskind's Perverse Vision. *Policy Review* 125:3–16.

Rosenzweig, Roy, and David Thelen. 1998. *The Presence of the Past: Popular Uses of History in American Life.* New York: Columbia University Press.

Roushanzamir, Elli, and Peggy Kreshel. 2001. Gloria and Anthony Visit a Plantation: History into Heritage at "Laura: A Creole Plantation." In *Slavery, Contested Heritage, and Thanatourism,* Graham Dann and A. V. Seaton, eds., pp. 177–200. New York: Haworth Press.

Rowat, Alison. 2002. Sites Best Left Unseen by the Tourist. *The Herald UK,* November 26.

Ruby, Jay. 2000. *Picturing Culture: Explorations of Film and Anthropology.* Chicago: University of Chicago Press.

Ruchelman, Leonard. 1977. *The World Trade Center: Politics and Policies of Skyscraper Development.* Syracuse, NY: Syracuse University Press.

Santino, Jack. 1992. Yellow Ribbons and Seasonal Flags: The Folk Assemblage of War. *The Journal of American Folklore* 105(415): 19–33.

Sather-Wagstaff, Joy. 2008. Picturing Experience: A Tourist-centred Perspective on Commemorative Historical Sites. *Tourist Studies: An International Journal* 8(1):77–103.

Schofield, John, William Gray Johnson, and Colleen M. Beck, eds. 2002. Introduction: Matériel Culture in the Modern World. In *Matériel Culture: The Archaeology of Twentieth-Century Conflict,* John Schofield, William Gray Johnson, and Colleen M. Beck, eds., pp. 1–8. London: Routledge.

Seaton, Anthony V. 1996. From Thanatopsis to Thanatourism: Guided by the Dark. *Journal of International Heritage Studies* 22:234–44.

———. 1999. War and Thanatourism: Waterloo 1815–1914. *Annals of Tourism Research* 26(1):130–58.

———. 2001. Sources of Slavery-Destinations of Slavery: The Silences and Disclosures of Slavery Heritage in the UK and US. In *Slavery, Contested Heritage, and Thanatourism*, Graham Dann and A. V. Seaton, eds., pp. 107–29. New York: Haworth Press.

Sellars, Richard W. 1990. Why Take a Trip to Bountiful—Won't Anaheim Do? Perception and Manipulation of the Historic Past. *Landscape* 30(3):14–19.

Sharpley, Richard, and Philip Stone. 2009. *The Darker Side of Travel: The Theory and Practice of Dark Tourism*. Bristol: Channel View Publications.

Shoval, Noam. 2000. Commodification and Theming of the Sacred: Changing Patterns of Tourist Consumption in the "Holy Land." In *New Forms of Consumption: Consumers, Culture, and Commodification*, Mark Gottdiener, ed., pp. 251–63. Lanham, MD: Rowman & Littlefield.

Simpson, David. 2006. *9/11: The Culture of Commemoration*. Chicago: University of Chicago Press.

Slade, Peter. 2003. Gallipoli Thanatourism: The Meaning of ANZAC. *Annals of Tourism Research* 30(4):779–94.

Sloane, David. 1991. The Last Great Necessity: Cemeteries in American History. Baltimore: Johns Hopkins University Press.

Smith, Johnathan Z. 1987. *To Take Place: Toward Theory in Ritual*. Chicago: University of Chicago Press.

Smith, Valene. 1989 [1977]. Introduction. In *Hosts and Guests: The Anthropology of Tourism*. Valene Smith, ed., pp. 1–14. Philadelphia: University of Pennsylvania Press.

———. 1996. War and Its Tourist Attractions. In *Tourism, Crime, and International Security Issues*, Abraham Pizam and Yoel Mansfeld, eds., pp. 247–64. Chichester: Wiley.

———. 1998. War and Tourism: An American Ethnography. *Annals of Tourism Research* 25(1):202–27.

Sobel, Rebekah. 2009. Connecting Cultural Identity and Place through Tourist Photograph: American Jewish Youth on a First Trip to Israel. In

The Framed World: Tourism, Tourists, and Photography. Mike Robinson and David Picard, eds., pp. 229–38. Burlington, VT: Ashgate.

Sontag, Susan. 1977. *On Photography*. New York: Farrar, Straus, and Giroux.

———. 1984. *On Longing: Narratives of the Miniature, the Gigantic, and Souvenir, and the Collection*. Baltimore: Johns Hopkins University Press.

Sorkin, Michael. 2003. *Starting from Ground Zero: Reconstructing Downtown New York*. New York: Routledge.

Stewart, Susan. 1984. *On Longing: Narratives of the Miniature, the Gigantic, and Souvenir, and the Collection*. Baltimore: Johns Hopkins University Press.

Stone, Philip. 2006. A Dark Tourism Spectrum: Toward a Typology of Death and Macabre Related Tourist Sites, Attractions and Exhibitions. *Tourism* 54(2):145–60.

Stone, Philip, and Richard Sharpley. 2008. Consuming Dark Tourism: A Thanatological Perspective. *Annals of Tourism Research*. 35(2):574–95.

Strange, Carolyn, and Michael Kempa. 2003. Shades of Dark Tourism: Alcatraz and Robben Island. *Annals of Tourism Research* 30(2):386–405.

Sturken, Marita. 1997. *Tangled Memories: The Vietnam War, the AIDS Epidemic, and the Politics of Remembering*. Berkeley and Los Angeles: University of California Press.

———. 1999. The Image as Memorial: Personal Photographs in Cultural Memory. In *The Familial Gaze*. Marianne Hirsch, ed., pp. 178–95. Hanover, NH: University Press of New England.

———. 2004. The Aesthetics of Absence: Rebuilding Ground Zero. *American Ethnologist* 31(3):311–25.

———. 2007. *Tourists of History: Memory, Kitsch, and Consumerism from Oklahoma City to Ground Zero*. Durham, NC: Duke University Press.

Taussig, Michael. 1997. *The Magic of the State*. New York: Routledge.

Taylor, Diana. 2005. *The Archive and the Repertoire: Performing Cultural Memory in the Americas*. Durham, NC: Duke University Press.

Todorov, Tzvetan. 1984. *Mikhail Bakhtin: The Dialogic Principle*. Minneapolis: University of Minnesota Press.

Trouillot, Michel-Rolph. 1991. Anthropology and the Savage Slot: The Poetics and Politics of Otherness. In *Recapturing Anthropology: Working in the Present*. Richard Fox, ed., pp. 17–44. Santa Fe, NM: School of American Research Press.

———. 1995. *Silencing the Past: Power and the Production of History*. Boston: Beacon.

Tuan, Yi-Fu. 1977. *Space and Place: The Perspectives of Experience*. Minneapolis: University of Minnesota Press.

Tunbridge, John, and Gregory Ashworth. 1996. *Dissonant Heritage: The Management of the Past as a Resource in Conflict*. Chichester: Wiley.

Turner, Victor. 1974. *Dramas, Fields, and Metaphors: Symbolic Action in Human Society*. Ithaca, NY: Cornell University Press.

Urry, John. 1995. *Consuming Places*. New York: Routledge.

———. 2002 [1990]. *The Tourist Gaze*. London: Sage.

Wallace, Tim. 2005. Tourism, Tourists, and Anthropologists at Work. *National Association for the Practice of Anthropology Bulletin* 23:1–26.

Watson, G. Llewellyn, and Joseph Kopachevsky. 1994. Interpretations of Tourism as Commodity. *Annals of Tourism Research* 21(3):643–60.

Watts, Linda. 2009. Reflecting Absence or Presence? Public Space and Historical Memory at Ground Zero. *Space and Culture* 12(4):412–18.

White, Geoffrey. 2004. National Subjects: September 11 and Pearl Harbor. *American Ethnologist* 31(3):293–310.

Williams, Paul. 2007. *Memorial Museums: The Global Rush to Commemorate Atrocities*. New York: Berg.

Yoneyama, Lisa. 1994. Taming the Memoryscape: Hiroshima's Urban Renewal. In *Remapping Memory: The Politics of TimeSpace*. Jonathan Boyarin, ed., pp. 99–135. Minneapolis: University of Minnesota Press.

Young, James. 1993. *The Texture of Memory: Holocaust Memorials and Meaning*. New Haven, CT: Yale University Press.

———. 2006. The Stages of Memory at Ground Zero. In *Religion, Violence, Memory, Place*. Oren Baruch Stier and J. Sawn Landers, eds., pp. 214–34. Bloomington: Indiana University Press.

Zolberg, Vera. 1998. Museums as Contested Sites of Remembrance: The Enola Gay Affair. In *Theorizing Museums: Representing Identity and Diversity in a Changing World.* Sharon MacDonald and Gordon Fyfe, eds., pp. 69–82. Oxford: Blackwell.

Zukin, Sharon. 2002. One World Trade Center. In *After the World Trade Center: Rethinking New York City.* Michael Sorkin and Sharon Zukin, eds., pp. 13–21. New York: Routledge.

Index

ABOUT THE AUTHOR

Joy Sather-Wagstaff is an assistant professor of anthropology at North Dakota State University. In addition to her 9/11 and Oklahoma City work, she has done research at and with colleagues at the United States Holocaust Memorial Museum on the effects of interactive antigenocide exhibits. Fascinated with vampires, medieval medicine, public executions in history, and other "dark" topics from quite a young age, her interests have influenced not only her scholarly research but also her teaching. Two of her favorite courses to teach are *Death and Dying* and *Disaster and Culture*.